Letts

Framework FOCUS

Shakespeare

Adrian Lockwood

Published by Letts Educational
The Chiswick Centre
414 Chiswick High Road
London W4 5TF

t 020 89963333
f 020 87428390
e mail@lettsed.co.uk
w www.letts-education.com

Letts Educational Limited is a division of Granada Learning Limited, part of Granada plc.

First published 2003

ISBN 1 84085 8761

For government guidance on internet safety for parents, please see:
http://safety.ngfl.gov.uk/parents

British Library Cataloguing in Publication Data
A catalogue record for this book is available from the British Library.

Developed and packaged by McLean Press Ltd

Commissioned by Helen Clark

Project management by Vicky Butt

Edited by Rosalind Horton

Cover design by bigtop, Bicester, UK

Internal design by bigtop, Bicester, UK

Illustrations by Linda Combi, Abigail Conway, Serena Curmi, Nick Duffy, Rosalind Hudson, Paul McCaffrey and Andrew Quelch

Production by PDQ

Printed and bound in the UK by Canale, Italy

Contents

Reviewing Key Stage 2

Aims

- To research the historical background of Shakespeare's life and times.
- To explore aspects of Elizabethan theatre.
- To remind yourselves how to read Shakespeare's English.

Starter session

You were introduced to some of Shakespeare's work in your primary school.

Here is a short exercise to test your memory and help you to become reacquainted with some facts about Shakespeare. Work with a partner to fill in the gaps. The answers are jumbled up in the box below.

Shakespeare was a famous _playwright_ who lived in the late _____ and early _____ centuries. He wrote both _plays_ and _comedies_ Although he grew up in Stratford-upon-Avon, he spent much of his career in the city of _London_. During some of that time theatres were actually _____ from the city.

Shakespeare's plays have been divided into three categories: _____, _____ and _____.

By the end of his life he had written _thirty-seven_ plays, the final one being _The Tempest_.

London   poems   Tragedies   playwright   plays   thirty-seven   William   sixteenth   banned
Comedies   seventeenth   The Tempest   Histories

- In pairs, make a list of reasons why some young people dislike reading Shakespeare.
- Feed your answers back to the class.
- As a class, discuss how Shakespeare could be made more popular with young people.

Introduction

It is often claimed that Shakespeare is the most famous playwright in the world. In the following sections you will remind yourself about aspects of his life, the Elizabethan theatre and how to read his verse.

Development

 **A** **DRAMA** SPEAKING AND LISTENING READING WRITING

Shakespeare's background

In groups, undertake a mini fact-finding project about Shakespeare's background and times. Your research should involve using the school library and perhaps the Internet. You will then use your information to produce a leaflet for younger children on facts about Shakespeare.

● First, choose one topic to research from the following:
   a Shakespeare's background and life in Stratford
   b Shakespeare's career in London
   c The background/story/characters for one of Shakespeare's plays.

● To do the research you will have to ask yourselves what other people might be interested in. You could start by preparing a list of questions to give your research some focus. Below are some starter questions for each section:
   a What is the date of Shakespeare's birth?
   What did Shakespeare's father do? What was his mother's name?
   Whom did Shakespeare marry?
   b Which group of actors did Shakespeare join in 1584?
   Name two of the famous actors.
   How many plays did Shakespeare write?
   c Roughly when was the play written?
   What information is there about key characters and themes?
   What happens?

Here are some useful websites:
www.shakespeare-online.com/
www.shakespeare.com/

The Elizabethan theatre

The theatre in Shakespeare's time looked and felt very different from a modern theatre. Look at the diagram below of the original Globe playhouse where some of Shakespeare's plays were performed.

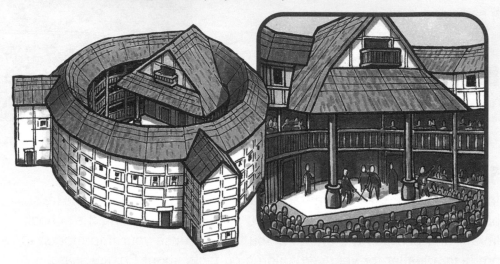

1 In pairs, look at the diagram and discuss the differences between the Globe theatre and a modern theatre. Consider how it looks, the technology, the audience, and so on.

2 Working in small groups, discuss the following statements about the Elizabethan theatre and decide if they are true or false:

   a The Globe could hold up to 3,000 people.
   b No special effects were possible.
   c The audience and sometimes the actors were soaked when it rained.
   d There were many female actors.
   e Audiences sometimes became restless and talked loudly through performances, occasionally shouting abuse at the performers.

3 You are now going to design a plan for the ultimate theatre of the future using the most modern technology. Consider the following:

   ● the shape of the stage (or perhaps it can take more than one shape!)
   ● where the audience will be
   ● what futuristic special effects might be possible, for example lasers, holograms, etc.
   ● include any other essential features that could be needed for the theatre, for example dressing rooms, props room, where the musicians will be, etc.
   ● a name for your ultra-modern theatre.

Reading Shakespeare

Reading Shakespeare's text can sometimes be difficult, but remember that the plays were written to be performed, not just read.

Use the following hints to help you in reading Shakespeare.

HINTS!

✳ Use the punctuation to indicate where you should pause.
✳ Don't pause at the end of a line unless the punctuation tells you to.

1 With a partner, read the following speech by the Prince in *Romeo and Juliet*. Each time you come to a punctuation pause, let your partner take over the reading.

> PRINCE: Rebellious subjects, enemies to peace, [...]
> Will they not hear? What ho! You men, you beasts!
> [...] Throw your mistemper'd weapons to the ground
> And hear the sentence of your moved prince.
>
> *[Act 1, scene 1, lines 81–86]*

HINTS!

✳ Think about how the character might be feeling.
✳ Emphasise the words that express the character's feelings.

2 In the speech above, the Prince is trying to stop a public battle taking place.
● In pairs, consider what he may be feeling.
● Reread each line, giving expression to the words showing his feelings.
● Add in the appropriate tone of voice, gestures and facial expressions to bring the piece alive.

Review

As a class, discuss what has helped you to feel more comfortable reading Shakespeare.

Discuss why it is important for young people to study Shakespeare.

A Midsummer Night's Dream

STUDYING CHARACTER

Aims

- To explore how Shakespeare creates characters through their actions and the way they speak and use language.
- To put yourself in the place of the characters and imagine their thoughts and emotions.

Starter session

We study people all the time in everyday life. Studying a character in a play uses many of the same techniques. Complete this activity to give you a starting point for looking at some of Shakespeare's characters.

- Imagine a new pupil has joined your English class. Working in pairs, make a list of all the things that will give you clues about this person's character, for example, how they walk, the way they react to the teacher, and so on.
- Compare your notes with another pair before feeding back to the class.
- Add to your list any other ideas from the feedback session.
- You may want to refer to your list later in the lesson.

Introduction

A Midsummer Night's Dream involves a host of strange and comical characters. Some of these are human and others are from the supernatural world of the fairies who live in the forest. The fairies are ruled over by Oberon and Titania, the king and queen of the fairy world.

Development

The following scene involves the meeting in the forest between Oberon and Titania, who have fallen out with each other over the ownership of an Indian boy.

In pairs, read the scene out loud. You can either choose one of the characters to read, or take it in turns to read a line at a time.

OBERON: Ill met by moonlight, proud Titania.

TITANIA: What, jealous Oberon! Fairies, skip hence;
I have forsworn his bed and company.

OBERON: Tarry, rash wanton; am not I thy lord?

TITANIA: Then I must be thy lady; but I know
When thou hast stolen away from fairy land [...]
Playing on pipes of corn, and versing love
To amorous Phillida. Why art thou here,
Come from the farthest step of India,
But that, forsooth, the bouncing Amazon,
Your buskin'd mistress and your warrior love,
To Theseus must be wedded [...]

OBERON: How canst thou thus, for shame, Titania,
Glance at my credit with Hippolyta,
Knowing I know thy love to Theseus? [...]

TITANIA: These are the forgeries of jealousy [...]

(Act 2, scene 1, lines 60–81)

1 In pairs, make notes on the following:

- Oberon and Titania are meant to be the king and queen of the fairies. What state do you think their marriage is in?
- Write down a word each for Oberon and Titania showing one aspect of their character. Is there a key line that might help?

2 With your partner, you will now attempt a short performance using only the first five lines, up to 'Then I must be thy lady'. The challenge is to convey a key element of the characters and their feelings. Consider the following:

- Which key words could you stress in each line to show the character's feelings?
- Oberon says, 'am not I thy lord?'. What do you think he is really trying to say to his wife?
- What tone of voice might Titania use to reply, 'Then I must be thy lady'? What aspect of her character comes across strongly here?

Get ready to perform for the rest of the class to see.

Review

- Now you have seen some of the other performances, what aspects of both characters have all the pairs agreed on in their performances? Discuss this as a class.
- Which pair gave the most convincing performance? Why were they successful?
- What would you change or improve on in your own performance to put across the characters more convincingly?

A Midsummer Night's Dream

THE FAIRY WORLD

Aims

- To explore how a writer's style creates a setting and atmosphere.
- To be able to comment on Shakespeare's choice of descriptive techniques.

Starter session

Much of the play is situated in the strange and magical fairy kingdom of the forest. Read the following description:

> Fairy: And I serve the Fairy Queen [...]
> The cowslips tall her pensioners be,
> In their gold coats spots you see;
> Those be rubies, fairy favours,
> In those freckles live their savours
> I must go seek some dew-drops here,
> And hang a pearl in every cowslip's ear.
>
> [Act 2, scene 1, lines 1, 8–15]

- In pairs, make a list of the main features of the fairy kingdom from the extract above.
- You have five minutes to draw a rough sketch of how you imagine the fairy kingdom. It must be from the fairies' point of view (remember their size).
- Now choose two features from your picture and write a line on each, describing them in a poetic way. One line must use a **simile**, and the other **alliteration**.

Introduction

The anger between the king and queen of the fairies, Oberon and Titania, has caused chaos in the fairy kingdom. Shakespeare creates this vision using various techniques:

- **imagery** – similes, **metaphors** and **personification**
- use of sounds – **alliteration**, **assonance**
- **emotive language**.

Development

DRAMA **SPEAKING AND LISTENING** **READING** **WRITING**

In groups of four, take turns to read out loud Titania's speech below.

TITANIA: Therefore the winds, piping to us in vain,   [Section 1]
As in revenge have suck'd up from the sea
Contagious fogs; which, falling in the land,
Hath every pelting river made so proud
That they have overborne their continents.
The ox hath therefore stretch'd his yoke in vain,
The ploughman lost his sweat, and the green corn
Hath rotted ere his youth attain'd a beard [...]
[...] the moon, the governess of floods,
Pale in her anger, washes all the air,
That rheumatic diseases do abound.
And thorough this distemperature we see   [Section 2]
The seasons alter: hoary-headed frosts
Fall in the fresh lap of the crimson rose;
And on old Hiems' thin and icy crown
An odorous chaplet of sweet summer buds
Is, as in mockery, set; the spring, the summer,
The childing autumn, angry winter, change
Their wonted liveries; and the mazed world,
By their increase, now knows not which is which.

[Act 2, Scene 1, lines 88–114]

1 Draw a rough sketch of the fairy kingdom using the detail from above. Write in the words and lines from the speech that have influenced you. Think about how this sketch will contrast with the one you did in the Starter session activity.

2 Divide your group of four into pairs and each pair take one of the sections of the speech.

- Decide which techniques Shakespeare has used to create the atmosphere of chaos and confusion (refer to the Introduction to remind yourself of the various techniques). Find as many quotations as you can to use as evidence. Example: 'contagious fogs' (*metaphor*) – 'contagious' suggests disease and the plague.
- Get back together as a group of four and compare your findings. What similarities have you found in Shakespeare's style?

Review

- Feed back to the class the results of your investigation. Which lines do you think are the most effective in creating the atmosphere?
- What are Shakespeare's techniques in this passage?

Homework

You are going to try and write eight more lines, either to add to the end of Titania's speech, or to the fairy's speech which you read for the Starter session activity. You must:

- sustain the setting and atmosphere for whichever speech you have chosen
- use at least one simile and metaphor
- use examples of alliteration, repetition or assonance
- attempt to use emotive words (for example, Shakespeare uses 'revenge', 'contagious', 'anger', and 'odorous').

A Midsummer Night's Dream

A SATIRE

Aims

- To understand that the views and attitudes of the characters are not always the same as the writer's.
- To see how aspects of Shakespeare's comedy have been influential to drama and literature through time.

Starter session

In *A Midsummer Night's Dream*, the comic character Bottom is an arrogant, meddling, foolish weaver who lives under the illusion that he is an accomplished actor.

- Make a list of your own Top Five all-time favourite film or TV comedies.
- Now take a favourite line, action, walk or facial expression from your chosen comedy and re-enact it for the class to enjoy.
- With a partner, make a list of things that you think make a successful comedy.

Introduction

While Bottom has been rehearsing a play in the forest, a mischievous fairy called Puck has put a spell on him, changing his head into that of a donkey's. Meanwhile, the jealous Oberon has the sleeping Titania spellbound, so that she will fall in love with the first living thing she sees when she wakes. The scene below shows what happens.

One of Shakespeare's most effective techniques for comedy was to allow the audience to know and see something that the characters were blind to. This is known as **dramatic irony**. The following scene is a perfect example of this.

[Re-enter BOTTOM with an ass's head]

QUINCE: O monstrous! O strange! We are haunted. […]
Fly, masters!

[Exeunt all but BOTTOM]

BOTTOM: I see their knavery: this is to make an ass of me, to fright me, if they could. But I will not stir from this place […] I will walk up and down here, and I will sing, that they shall hear I am not afraid.   *[Sings]*

TITANIA: What angel wakes me from my flowery bed?
[Bottom sings]
[…] I pray thee, gentle mortal, sing again:
Mine ear is much enamour'd of thy note;
So is mine eye enthralled to thy shape;
And thy fair virtue's force perforce doth move me
On the first view to say, to swear, I love thee.

BOTTOM: Methinks, mistress, you should have little reason for that. And yet, to say the truth, reason and love keep little company together nowadays. […]

TITANIA: Thou art as wise as thou art beautiful […]
And I do love thee: therefore go with me.

[Act 3, scene 1, lines 114–148]

This scene is very similar to the plot of many modern romantic comedies, for example, the two incompatible people who overcome all obstacles and finally find true love together, or the character who is blinded by love.

Development

DRAMA   SPEAKING AND LISTENING   READING   WRITING

1 In groups of four discuss:
- What makes this a comic scene?
- What kind of writing, or **genre**, do you think Shakespeare was making fun of?
- Which lines are we obviously meant to laugh at? Find five examples.
- In what ways do the characters' perception of the scene differ from the audience's?
- Can you think of a scene in a modern film, novel or play with a similar idea?

2 *A Midsummer Night's Dream* is a **satire** of romantic love. The romance in this scene is not meant to be taken seriously. Instead, we are supposed to laugh at it.
- In pairs, write a short scene that **satirises** a particular type of writing, either romance or tragedy.
- Use some of Shakespeare's techniques, for example language and emotions that are hugely exaggerated, dramatic irony and a comic plot idea.
- Keep it simple – only use a small number of characters (two or three).

3 In your pairs, act out an extract from your script that is clearly meant to be **satirical** (which makes fun of your chosen genre).
- Act it in an exaggerated way to emphasise the comedy.
- Speak your lines clearly and in a way that highlights how ludicrous it is.

Review

- Try to explain to the class how you have used dramatic irony. How are your own views and attitudes different from those of your characters?

YEAR 7 | UNIT 4

A Midsummer Night's Dream

THE LOVERS' STORY

Aims

- To understand how a writer develops and structures key ideas.
- To examine and comment on the ending.

Starter session

A Midsummer Night's Dream begins with conflict: Egeus disapproves of Lysander, with whom his daughter, Hermia, is in love. Instead, he has given Demetrius his consent to marry Hermia and wants Theseus, Duke of Athens, to enforce this.

Helena, one of Hermia's friends, is heartbroken, as she is in love with Demetrius!

Read the extract on the right.

- Discuss as a class what your feelings are about how Egeus treats his daughter.
- In small groups, try to predict five different possibilities for what will happen in this story.
- How might it develop and what different endings might there be?

> EGEUS: Full of vexation come I, with complaint
> Against my child, my daughter Hermia.
> Stand forth Demetrius [...]
> This man hath my consent to marry her.
> Stand forth, Lysander [...]
> With cunning hast thou filch'd my daughter's heart,
> Turn'd her obedience (which is due to me)
> To stubborn harshness. And, my gracious Duke [...]
> I beg the ancient privilege of Athens:
> As she is mine, I may dispose of her;
> Which shall be either to this gentleman,
> Or to her death, according to our law.
>
> *[Act 1, scene 1, lines 22–44]*

Introduction

The **plots** and **sub-plots** of Shakespeare's plays use the standard five-part story **structure**:

1 introduction   **2** development   **3** complication   **4** crisis   **5** resolution.

Development

DRAMA   **SPEAKING AND LISTENING**   *READING*   *WRITING*

1 Below is a series of summary snippets for the lovers' sub-plot of *A Midsummer Night's Dream*. In small groups, decide where each one fits into the five-part story structure (above).

Make sure you read them *all* first.

a Helena, madly in love with Demetrius, tells him that Lysander and Hermia have run away.

b In the wood, Oberon observes how unkindly Demetrius treats Helena. He orders Puck to enchant Demetrius so that he falls in love with her.

c Egeus tries to force Hermia to marry Demetrius instead of Lysander.

d Puck mistakenly puts the spell on Lysander, then enchants Demetrius too!

e Helena thinks they are playing a cruel joke on her.

f Theseus and Egeus find the lovers asleep in the wood. When they wake Demetrius, still under the spell, declares his true love for Helena. Theseus announces their wedding at the Temple.

g Demetrius pursues the two lovers into the wood followed by the lovesick Helena.

h Hermia and Lysander escape into the forest.

i Both men, now obsessed with Helena, fight over her.

j Oberon removes the spell from Lysander. The lovers fall asleep.

2 Now see if you can match the quotes on the next page to the correct plot summary snippet from question 1 (occasionally there may be more than one quotation for each plot point).

i	HELENA:	I am your spaniel; and, Demetrius, The more you beat me, I will fawn on you.
	DEMETRIUS:	[...] I am sick when I do look on thee.
ii	THESEUS:	Fair lovers, you are fortunately met; [...] For in the temple, by and by, with us These couples shall eternally be knit.
iii	DEMETRIUS:	[To Theseus] The object and pleasure of mine eye, Is only Helena. To her my lord, Was I betroth'd ere I saw Hermia.
iv	OBERON:	[To Puck] What hast thou done? Thou hast mistaken quite, And laid the love-juice on some true love's sight.
v	HELENA:	O spite! O hell! I see you are all bent To set against me for your merriment.
vi	OBERON:	[To Puck] A sweet Athenian lady is in love With a disdainful youth; anoint his eyes; But do it when the next thing he espies May be the lady. [...] that he may prove More fond on her than she upon her love.
vii	HELENA:	I will go tell him of fair Hermia's flight; Then to the wood will he tomorrow night Pursue her...

3 In your group, construct a series of five dramatic still-life pictures retelling the lovers' plot in *A Midsummer Nights Dream*. You will present this to the class.

- Some of you may have to play several roles to cover all the characters in the story.
- Think carefully about how to portray clearly the events and the characters' feelings.
- Provide a short title for each picture.
- Consider the ending and your final picture. Is it a comfortable ending?
- Remember that Demetrius is only in love with Helena because he is still under Puck's spell. How can this be conveyed to your audience?

Review

- In pairs, compare the lovers' plot in the play with your predictions in the Starter session activity. How accurate were you? Which elements were similar? Was your ending a happy one?
- As a class, comment on the ending of the play. Was it entirely predictable? What about Demetrius, who is still under Puck's spell at the end? Do we still believe that it is an entirely happy ending?

Homework

Invent the plot for your own romance, which is unpredictable and doesn't have the expected ending:

- Show the plot in six to eight parts.
- Try your best to defy expectations – it isn't as easy as it sounds!

UNIT 5

The Tempest

THE SHIPWRECK (DRAMATIC OPENINGS)

Aims

- To visualise a Shakespearean scene.
- To comment on the atmosphere and mood of the scene.

Starter session

The opening scene of any play, film or novel is crucial.

- Working in pairs, discuss any memorable openings to a film you have seen. Describe what happened and consider why these openings were effective.
- Now make a list of the things a playwright may want to establish at the beginning of the play:
  - What effect might the playwright want the opening to have on the audience?
  - Consider other elements such as character, atmosphere and plot.
- Feed back your ideas to the class.

Introduction

A dramatic opening is crucial in capturing the audience's attention. It keeps them in their seats with the promise that they will be treated to more later.

The Tempest opens with a ship carrying Alonso (the King of Naples), Antonio (the Duke of Milan) and Sebastian, Ferdinand and Gonzalo (other high dignitaries). They are caught in a violent storm that threatens to destroy the ship, while the crewmen work desperately to keep it under control.

The **tension** in the scene comes through the drama of the storm and the conflict between the **high** and **low status** characters (the dignitaries and crewmen).

Development

Read the following scene. Try to **visualise** how it would look on stage or film.

On a ship at sea; a tempestuous noise of thunder and lightning heard. Enter a Shipmaster and Boatswain.

MASTER: [...]speak to th' mariners. Fall to't yarely or we run ourselves aground. Bestir, bestir! [*Exit*]

Enter Mariners

BOATSWAIN: Heigh, my hearts;
[...] Take in the topsail. Tend to the master's whistle!

Enter Alonso, Sebastian, Antonio, Ferdinand, Gonzalo and others.

ALONSO: Good boatswain, have care. Where's the master? Play the men!

BOATSWAIN: I pray now, keep below!

ANTONIO: Where is the master, boatswain?

BOATSWAIN: Do you not hear him? You mar our labour.
Keep your cabins! You do assist the storm.

GONZALO: Nay, good, be patient.

BOATSWAIN: When the sea is. Hence. What cares these roarers for the name of king? To cabin! Silence! Trouble us not.

GONZALO: Good, yet remember whom thou hast aboard.

BOATSWAIN: None that I more love than myself [...]
Down with the topmast! Yare! Lower, lower! Bring her to try with maincourse. [*A cry within*] A plague upon this howling. [...]

Re-enter Sebastian, Antonio and Gonzalo.

Yet again? What do you here? [...] Have you a mind to sink?

SEBASTIAN: A pox o'your throat, you bawling, blasphemous, incharitable dog.

BOATSWAIN: Work you, then.

ANTONIO: Hang, cur [...] We are less afraid to be drowned than thou art.

[*Act 1, scene 1, lines 3–43*]

1 In small groups, discuss how the dialogue makes the scene dramatic:
   ● Which lines suggest the desperation of the crew?
   ● Which lines show the conflict between the crew and the dignitaries?
   ● The boatswain is low status and the passengers are royalty, therefore high status, but what happens to the status of these characters through the scene?

2 Imagine you are a film-maker directing the opening of *The Tempest*. **Visualise** the scene carefully. Put together a detailed storyboard to illustrate how you will convey the tension and drama of the scene.
   ● Use eight boxes with illustrations and lay them out like a comic. Leave two lines below each one for dialogue.
   ● Make notes on the type of camera shot you want, for example **long shot**, **close-up**, **panning**.
   ● Include sound effects and type of music.
   ● What special effects will be necessary?
   ● Include some of the lines of dialogue from above to highlight the tension between the characters.

Review

In small groups, share the ideas from your film storyboards. Discuss what you were trying to put across and how you achieved that.

As a class, discuss how directing the opening of a stage production of *The Tempest* would be different from a film version. What other factors would you have to consider?

Homework
● Do a storyboard for the beginning of the play version. Don't forget to consider the way live theatre differs from a film.

The Tempest

PROSPERO, THE RULER

Aims

- To understand a character through what is implied in what they say ('reading between the lines').

Starter session

Prospero rules over an enchanted island in *The Tempest*. He uses his magical powers to create order and control his few subjects.

- Construct a spider diagram of all the qualities a good ruler should have. Include at least three main principles you would use to rule by, for example, fairness.
- Working in pairs, compare your ideas.
- As a class, discuss what qualities you have found most important in a ruler. Do you know any real-life examples of good or bad rulers?

Introduction

Prospero was the Duke of Milan before he was overthrown secretly by his greedy brother, Sebastian, then set adrift at sea to die with his infant daughter, Miranda.

Luckily, a kindly counsellor, Gonzalo, helped Prospero by providing him with food and his books of magic as he was cast away in an old, sinking boat. Prospero and Miranda are eventually washed onto an island, which Prospero claims as his own. Prospero is a **complex character**, who believes himself to be right and virtuous, although the audience often sees another side to his personality.

Development

Read the following extract in which Prospero recounts to Miranda how he was overthrown.

PROSPERO: Obey and be attentive [...]
    Twelve year since, Miranda [...]
    Thy father was the Duke of Milan and
    A prince of power. [...]
MIRANDA: What foul play had we that we came from thence? [...]
PROSPERO: My brother and thy uncle, called Antonio [...]
    [...] he, whom next thyself
    Of all the world I loved, and to him put
    The manage of my state [...]
    And Prospero the prime Duke, being so reputed
    In dignity, and for the liberal arts
    Without a parallel; those being all my study,
    The government I cast upon my brother
    And to my state grew stranger, being transported
    And rapt in secret studies.
    [...] in my false brother
    Awaked an evil nature [...]
    [...] as great
    As my trust was, which had indeed no limit [...]

[Act 1, scene 2, lines 37–96]

1 Draw a sketch of Prospero as the ruler of the island. Consider what might show his authority and magical powers.

2 In a small group, make notes around your sketches on the following points:

- Prospero's feelings about his brother, remembering that there may be mixed feelings. Give short quotes as evidence.
- What did Prospero spend his time doing as ruler?
- Was Prospero a good ruler? What were his weaknesses?

3 Read the extract below, which shows how Prospero rules over Ariel, his spirit servant.

PROSPERO: What is't thou canst demand?
ARIEL: My liberty.
    [...] Remember I have done thee worthy service [...]
PROSPERO: Dost thou forget
    From what a torment I did free thee? [...]
ARIEL: I do not, sir.
PROSPERO: Thou liest, malignant thing; hast thou forgot
    The foul witch Sycorax [...]
    She did confine thee,
    [...] Into a cloven pine [...]
    Imprisoned thou didst painfully remain
    A dozen years [...]
    If thou more murmur'st, I will rend an oak
    And peg thee in his knotty entrails till
    Thou hast howled away twelve winters.
ARIEL: Pardon, master [...]

[Act 1, scene 2, lines 244–97]

In pairs, discuss what method Prospero uses over Ariel, one of his closest subjects.

- What does Ariel desire?
- How does Prospero's response to Ariel make him appear as a ruler?
- Why do you think Prospero reacts so harshly to Ariel?

4 Now add the points you have just discussed to your sketch of Prospero.

Review

As a class, discuss what makes Prospero a complex character.

- As the ruler of the island, how does he differ from the perfect ruler discussed in the Starter session activity?
- Do you think Prospero sees himself as a bad ruler?

The Tempest

CALIBAN, THE 'SAVAGE' MONSTER?

Aims

- To understand how the attitudes or views of some of the characters are not necessarily those of the writer.
- To **empathise** with (put yourself in the place of) one of the characters.
- To improvise and role-play some of the key issues and characters.

Starter session

Prospero sees Caliban as a savage monster. List the characteristics that you would normally associate with a monster. Consider:

- What are monsters are supposed to do?
- What feelings might monsters have?
- What does the word 'savage' suggest?

Feed back some of your ideas to the class.
Are there any real-life monsters?

Introduction

Caliban is a native of the island and his mother, Sycorax the witch, ruled there before Prospero's arrival. Caliban began by helping Prospero before he was turned into a slave for trying to rape Miranda, Prospero's daughter. Because of this act, Caliban is seen as evil and savage.

However, Shakespeare has created a complex character, as Caliban sometimes defies our expectations of a 'monster'. Shakespeare does this by using a technique known as **juxtaposing**, which means that he shows us contrasting aspects of Caliban's character in different scenes allowing us to understand him better.

Development

Read the following extracts, which reveal Caliban's feelings and how Prospero treats him.

EXTRACT **A**

PROSPERO: What ho, slave! Caliban,
　　　　　[…] Come forth I say, there's other business for thee.
　　　　　[Caliban does not enter]
　　　　　Thou poisonous slave, got by the devil himself.
　　　　　[Enter Caliban]
CALIBAN: […] A southwest blow on ye
　　　　　And blister you all o'er.
PROSPERO: For this, be sure, tonight thou shalt have cramps,
　　　　　Side-stitches that shall pen thy breath up […]
CALIBAN: […] This island's mine by Sycorax my mother,
　　　　　Which thou tak'st from me. When thou cam'st first,
　　　　　Thou strok'st me and made much of me […]
　　　　　And then I loved thee […]
　　　　　Cursed be I that did so!
PROSPERO: Thou most lying slave […]
　　　　　I have used thee
　　　　　(Filth as thou art) with humane care […]
　　　　　Till thou didst seek to violate
　　　　　The honour of my child […]
　　　　　Fetch us in fuel […]
　　　　　If thou neglect'st […]
　　　　　I'll rack thee with old cramps,
　　　　　Fill all thy bones with aches, make thee roar.

　　　　　　　　　[Act 1, scene 2, lines 312–70]

EXTRACT **B**

CALIBAN: Be not afeard. The isle is full of noises,
　　　　　Sounds and sweet airs that give delight and hurt not.
　　　　　Sometimes a thousand twangling instruments
　　　　　Will hum about mine ears; and sometime voices,
　　　　　That if I then had waked after long sleep,
　　　　　Will make me sleep again.

　　　　　　　　　[Act 3, scene 2, lines 135–9]

1 In pairs, pick out a selection of key lines or phrases from Extract A that show the relationship between Caliban and Prospero.

- What method does Prospero use to make Caliban obey him?
- Why does Caliban feel he has been treated unjustly?
- Look at Extract B. How do Caliban's language and attitude differ here?
- What aspect of Caliban's personality is revealed here?

2 In small groups, improvise a talk show interview with Caliban and Prospero. Your main objective is to show the different sides of Caliban's personality.

- Have a theme for the show, for example 'Monster, or Misunderstood?' or 'Is he a Savage?'. This should be mentioned in the introduction to the show.
- You need at least four characters: a host, Caliban, Prospero and Miranda. Try to consider the feelings of the different characters.
- Consider your character's body language and how he or she would speak. For example, *Caliban: speaks angrily, defiantly; may be quite energetic, but also fearful of Prospero; he could show a rational, reasonable and well-spoken side of his character.*

Review

Perform your improvisations to the class, emphasising the differing sides to Caliban's personality.

As a class, discuss what makes Caliban a complex character. Consider how you are meant to feel about him.

Homework

- Caliban is Prospero's slave. Research and make notes on the conditions slaves lived under in the sixteenth and seventeenth centuries. Start by seeing what books there are in your school library on the subject of slavery. You might also like to try out the following website: **www.spartacus.schoolnet.co.uk/slavery.htm**

The Tempest

AND EXPLORATION

Aims

- To understand why some texts have been particularly significant through history.
- To distinguish between the writer's views and those of the characters.

Starter session

In the sixteenth century, European explorers and philosophers believed that near the Americas and West Indies there existed a 'New World', or 'Golden World', which they believed to be a perfect place. They set out on perilous voyages to find this elusive land and its peoples.

Read the following extract written in 1555 from *The Decades of the New World or West India*.

'The inhabitants of these Islands have been ever so used to live at liberty, in play and pastime, that they can hardly away with the yoke of servitude, which they attempt to shake off by all means they may. [...] Among these simple souls, a few clothes serve the naked [...] and [they] have not the use of pestiferous money [...]
They seem to live in that golden world [...] wherein men lived simply and innocently without enforcement of laws, without quarrelling [...]
They are content with so little.'

The writer believes this is a perfect society. In pairs, carry out the following activities:

- List what he considers to be the best features of this society.
- Can you find what clues he gives about what he despises in his own country?

Introduction

During the late sixteenth century, beautiful exotic lands and their native inhabitants were discovered by European explorers searching for the perfect world. However, as time went on, this dream was shattered. The Europeans often used their advanced technology, weapons or riches to overpower the native inhabitants and take these lands from them. The natives were sometimes taken and sold as slaves.

In *The Tempest*, Shakespeare gives us a glimpse of the reality of the so-called 'Golden World'. Prospero is washed ashore on an enchanted island and goes on to enslave its inhabitants, Caliban and Ariel, for his own use.

Development

DRAMA   **SPEAKING AND LISTENING**   **READING**   **WRITING**

1 Consider what would be your perfect world.
- List the things that you would try to get rid of or ban, for example drugs, poverty and so on.
- Give three key words to describe your perfect society, for example kind, cooperative and so on.
- Invent a short but effective motto for your land, which says something about your ideals or principles, for example 'Strength in Togetherness', 'Everyone is Equal'.

Feed back your ideas to the class.
As a class, discuss:

- Is a perfect world possible or realistic?
- What aspects of human nature make a perfect society difficult to achieve?

2 Read the following extract where Trinculo, a jester who is shipwrecked on the island, discovers the native Caliban, who is hiding in fear underneath a garment, believing Trinculo to be a spirit sent to torment him.

Although Trinculo's character is intended as comedy relief for the play, Shakespeare also uses him **symbolically** to put across the attitude and behaviour of the Europeans towards the native inhabitants of the 'New World'.

TRINCULO: What have we here, a man or a fish? Dead or alive? A fish: he smells like a fish [...] A strange fish! Were I in England now (as once I was) and had but this fish painted, not a holiday fool there but would give a piece of silver. There would this monster make a man; any strange beast there makes a man. When they will not give a doit to relieve a lame beggar, they will lay out ten to see a dead Indian [...] this is no fish, but an islander [...]

[Enter STEPHANO singing]
          [...]
STEPHANO: This is some monster of the isle, with four legs [...] If I can recover him and keep him tame, I will not take too much for him! He shall pay for him that hath him, and that soundly.

          [Act 2, scene 2 lines 24–78]

3 In groups, discuss the following:

- Find the phrases that both Stephano and Trinculo use to refer to Caliban. What does this tell you about their attitude towards him?
- What do both characters hope they can get by using him?
- It's difficult to know exactly what Shakespeare thought, but what point might he have been making about the Europeans and their treatment of the native inhabitants? Do you think Shakespeare agrees with Stephano and Trinculo's behaviour?
- How might a sixteenth-century audience, who knew nothing of foreigners, react to this scene? Would their reaction be the same as yours?

4 Consider how Shakespeare might have felt about the issue of slavery and the way the natives of the New World were used and treated by the Europeans.

Imagine you are Shakespeare writing a letter to 'The Elizabethan Times', a local newspaper, outlining your views about this issue. Think about:

- the points you would make to protest against it
- the feelings you would express
- what you think should be done about the situation.

Review

Read the class an extract from your letter that makes a particularly strong point.

If Stephano and Trinculo's views are not necessarily the same as Shakespeare's, why are they represented in the play? What purpose do they serve?

What issues might Shakespeare write about in today's world?

Writing about Shakespeare's plays

Aims

- To write a formal, structured response to one of Shakespeare's plays, focusing on a key issue and character.

Starter session

Test your perceptive abilities in reading using the following passage. Try to find clues about the characters.

She knew she was late. It meant trouble. She could feel it coming and just her luck that it was Smithers' class.

The door to the classroom opened a fraction, slowly. The hinges seemed to shriek sending a sick, stabbing feeling into her stomach. The class, rigid with silence, dared not turn to see who this unfortunate soul was – but the teacher did. Mr Smithers stood perfectly still, his dark eyes pinning the girl to the wall. She froze. Her insides disintegrating. It wasn't her fault, of all mornings her mother had …

'Kerry Jones, what a surprise. It's usually traditional to turn up at the *beginning* of a lesson', he hissed softly.

The class sniggered. Traitors, she thought.

She said, 'It wasn't my fault, my mother …'

It was then his eyes expanded in fury; he bellowed so loudly that the class bolted upright, 'SIT DOWN! NOW! I'm not interested in what …'

She never heard the end of that sentence. The last thing she remembered was running from the class. Crying. Knowing her mother had done it again.

Point   *Explanation*   *Evidence*

- In pairs, list what you learn about Kerry and Mr Smithers.
- Find short quotes to support your ideas.
- Feed back your ideas to the class.

Introduction

In this lesson you are going to write a short formal essay about the character of Caliban from *The Tempest*. You will sometimes need to refer to past lessons where you have studied his character (Units 7 and 8). In studying character, remember to think about:

- their thoughts and feelings
- how they treat other people
- what they say
- how they speak to others
- how others feel about them
- how they are treated.

Your essay will have to be written in a **formal** manner using paragraphs. You will be asked in each paragraph to:

- make an important point
- give an explanation for it (develop your idea)
- present the evidence (often a quote) to support your point.

Here is an example of a short paragraph using the text in the Starter session activity:

I think that Mr Smithers is a strict teacher with a bad temper. [Point]
The way the rest of the class are silent and dare not turn around when Kerry enters suggests this. Kerry also seems to be terrified when he first stares then speaks to her. [Explanation]
The text shows this when it says: 'She froze. Her insides disintegrating'. [Evidence]

Development

DRAMA **SPEAKING AND LISTENING** READING **WRITING**

1 Working with a partner, create a spidergram as you brainstorm what you remember about Caliban. Here is a model to get you started:

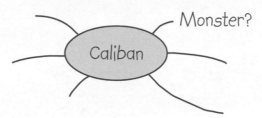

2 Share your answers with the class.

3 The title of your essay will be 'My Impressions of Caliban' (*The Tempest*). Your essay should be approximately 500 words long.

- Use the following points to help structure your essay:
  - Introduction – explain what your essay will be about.
  - Describe how Prospero treats Caliban and explain why.
  - Explain what Stephano and Trinculo would like to do to Caliban.
  - Write about Caliban's speech in which he talks about the sounds of the island and what it reveals about him.
  - Explain what makes Caliban a complex character.
  - Conclusion – say what your feelings are about how Caliban is treated. Does he deserve this treatment or do you have mixed feelings?

    Each of these should be a paragraph including a **point**, explanation and **evidence**.

- Make sure you pick suitable quotes as evidence for the points you are making. Use the extracts in Units 7 and 8 to find your quotations.

- The openings of the first two paragraphs are provided below. You can use these or think up you own:

  Introduction: In this essay I will be writing about …
  Paragraph 1: Prospero treats Caliban as if he is …

Review

- Read out an example from your essay that shows *point*, *explanation* and *evidence* being used.

Shakespeare in performance

Aims

- To explore various aspects of live theatre.

Starter session

Below you will find a list of things that a director must consider in planning a live performance if it is to be successful.

In groups, imagine you are putting on a performance and time is running short: put the elements below in order of priority, with the most important at the top of the list and the least important at the end.

Lighting   Actors delivering lines   Sound effects

Where the audience sit   Staging

Costumes   Scenery and stage design

Getting actors in character

Actors knowing their cues   Props

Actors projecting their voices

Refreshments for the audience

Feed back your results to the class. What was at the top of your list and what was at the bottom? What factors influenced your decisions?

Was the task as simple as it first appeared? What made it either easy or difficult?

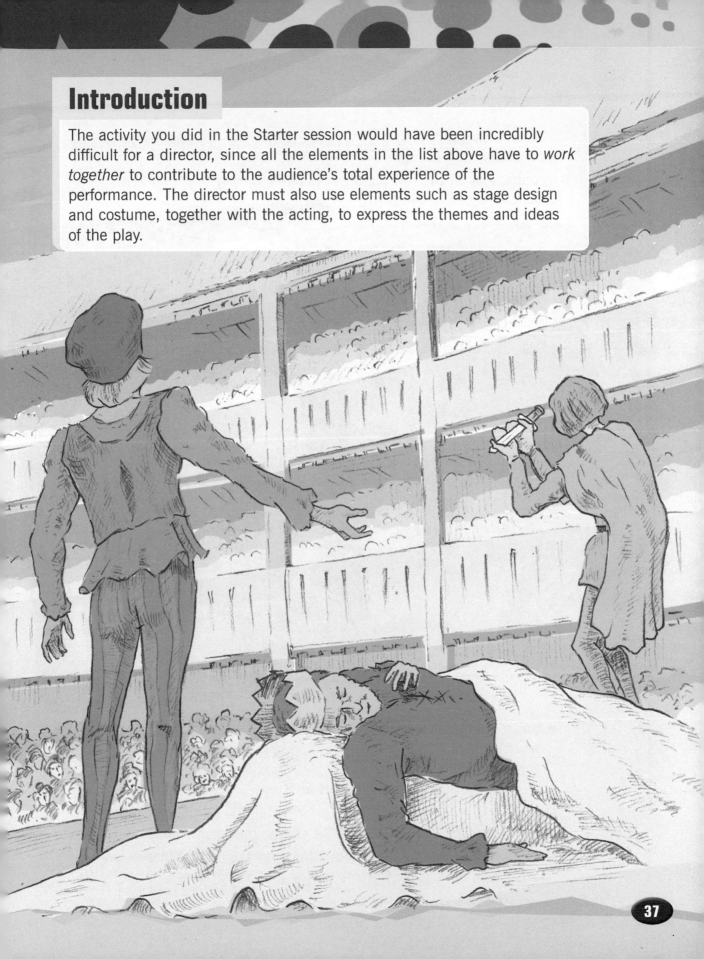

Introduction

The activity you did in the Starter session would have been incredibly difficult for a director, since all the elements in the list above have to *work together* to contribute to the audience's total experience of the performance. The director must also use elements such as stage design and costume, together with the acting, to express the themes and ideas of the play.

Development

1 In pairs, look at the two pictures of Caliban below from different productions of *The Tempest*.

©Joe Cocks Studio Collection, Shakespeare Centre Library, Stratford-upon-Avon

©Reg Wilson Collection, Royal Shakespeare Company

- Using your knowledge of Caliban from the previous lessons, discuss what the two directors were attempting to put across to the audience about his character.
- What similarities and differences are there?

2 Costumes and make-up are crucial for telling the audience something about a character, for example their **status**, role, personality, and so on.

- Look at the costume design for Titania on the right. What detail has been included to give the impression that she is queen of the fairies?

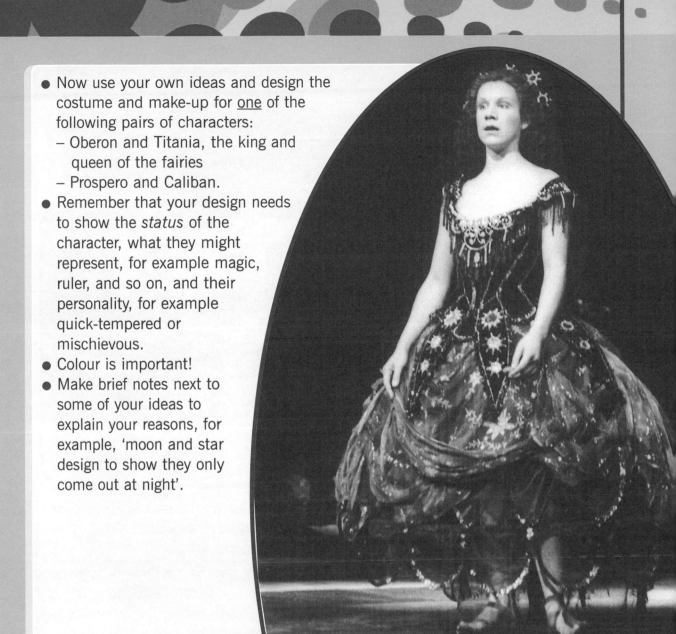

- Now use your own ideas and design the costume and make-up for <u>one</u> of the following pairs of characters:
  - Oberon and Titania, the king and queen of the fairies
  - Prospero and Caliban.
- Remember that your design needs to show the *status* of the character, what they might represent, for example magic, ruler, and so on, and their personality, for example quick-tempered or mischievous.
- Colour is important!
- Make brief notes next to some of your ideas to explain your reasons, for example, 'moon and star design to show they only come out at night'.

©Joe Cocks Studio Collection, Shakespeare Centre Library, Stratford-upon-Avon

Review

Compare your costume and make-up designs with a partner. What are the similarities and differences?

Feed your ideas back to the class and show them your pictures.

What importance do you think costume design may have in a live performance?

Class project

You are going to design and make a stage set for either the fairy world of the forest in *A Midsummer Night's Dream* or the enchanted island in *The Tempest*. You will have a week of English lessons to do this.

©Joe Cocks Studio Collection, Shakespeare Centre Library, Stratford-upon-Avon

- Look at this set design for the fairy world using the idea of a scrapyard instead of a forest. Is this what you would have expected? What suggests a magical fairy world in this design?

- Be as imaginative as possible. The setting can be anything or anywhere as long as it fits in with the ideas of the play. It can be modern, out of this world, realistic or surreal. Visit some websites on the Internet based on the theatre to give you ideas. The following are just a few suggestions to get you started:

  The International Theatre Design Archive – **www.siue.edu/ITDA/y.html**

  The Royal Shakespeare Company – **www.rsc.org.uk**

  The National Theatre – **www.nationaltheatre.org.uk**

- Decide on the shape of your stage:
  it can be 'theatre-in-the-round' (circular), a thrust stage (which comes out into the audience so they sit on all three sides of it) or a traditional stage.

- Make a detailed drawing of your stage design and label the features you have included.

- Decide what materials you will require to make the miniature model of your stage.

The Taming of the Shrew

KATHERINA, THE SHREW

Aims

- To examine the character of Katherina, and her relationship with other characters.
- To use role-play as a way of understanding characters and issues.

Starter session

A good deal of *The Taming of the Shrew* is about the relationship between two sisters and between a parent and child.

In pairs, write a short script of a typical argument between:

- either an older brother/sister and younger brother/sister
- or a parent and a teenage son or daughter.

Try to make the issue they are arguing about, and the attitudes and feelings of the characters, sound authentic. Now present a dramatic reading of the script to the class.

As a class, discuss what some of the issues are that cause family arguments:

- Why do brothers and sisters argue?
- What causes tension between parents and their children?

Introduction

Baptista Minola is a wealthy gentleman of Padua (a city in Italy) but he is at the end of his tether! He has two daughters: Bianca, who is the younger, and is kind and fair; and Katherina, the older daughter, who terrorises her family and anyone who crosses her path. To the men of Padua, Katherina is 'stark mad' and a 'devil'!

Development

DRAMA   SPEAKING AND LISTENING   READING   WRITING

The following scene shows an argument between Bianca and the 'shrewish' Katherina, who has tied her sister's hands together and demands to know about her many suitors.

BIANCA: Good sister, wrong me not, nor wrong yourself,
To make a [...] slave of me [...]
Unbind my hands [...]

KATHERINA: Of all thy suitors here I charge thee tell
Whom thou lov'st best [...]

BIANCA: Believe me, sister, of all the men alive
I never yet beheld that special face
Which I could fancy more than any other.

KATHERINA: Minion, thou liest. Is't not Hortensio?

BIANCA: If you affect him, sister [...]
I'll plead for you myself but you shall have him.

KATHERINA: O then [...] you fancy riches more.
You will have Gremio to keep you fair.

BIANCA: Is it for him you do envy me so? [...]
You have but jested with me all this while.
I prithee, sister Kate, untie my hands.

KATHERINA: If that be jest, then all the rest was so.
[Strikes her]
[Enter Baptista]

BAPTISTA: [...] Bianca, stand aside. Poor girl, she weeps [...]
Why dost thou wrong her that did ne'er wrong thee?

KATHERINA: Her silence flouts me, and I'll be reveng'd.
[Flies after Bianca]

BAPTISTA: What, in my sight? Bianca, get thee in.
[Exit Bianca]

KATHERINA: [...] Now I see
She is your treasure, she must have a husband,
I must dance barefoot on her wedding-day [...]
I will go sit and weep,
Till I can find some occasion for revenge.

BAPTISTA: Was ever gentleman thus griev'd as I?

[Act 2, scene 1, lines 1–37]

1 In a group of three, imagine you are family counsellors. Discuss:

- How would you describe Katherina and Bianca's relationship?
- What does Katherina want to know from Bianca?
- How effective is Baptista in dealing with Katherina?
- At the end of the extract, how does Katherina feel, and why?
- How are Katherina and Bianca different?

2 In your group, role-play the scene in modern English. Be prepared to perform to the class.

3 Imagine you are Baptista. Write a letter to a family counsellor outlining your distress about your daughters.

- Explain the situation between your daughters.
- Describe Katherina's behaviour.
- Include what you, as the father, have tried to do.
- Say what you think the problem with Katherina might be.
- What would you like to happen?

Review

In pairs, find quotes from the extract that show why Katherina might behave towards Bianca in the way that she does.

As a class, discuss what you think might help the situation? Are there strategies that can be used to ease the tensions?

Homework

Imagine that you are a family counsellor and you have received Baptista's letter about his daughters. Reply to his letter and include the following information:

- your ideas about what makes Katherina behave so badly
- any strategies or solutions for dealing with her.

The Taming of the Shrew

MARRIAGE

Aims

- To explore how texts reflect the attitudes and ideas of the time in which they are written.
- To recognise some key themes common in significant literature through the ages.

Starter session

The Taming of the Shrew is partly about men's and women's attitudes to marriage.

Your class is going to conduct a survey about your views to these issues. Your teacher will allocate three sections of the room for you to go to depending on your opinion on a series of statements. The three zones are:

AGREE   **DISAGREE**   **NEUTRAL (NOT SURE)**

When your teacher reads a statement, you must go and stand in the zone that shows your opinion.

Make up your own mind – don't be influenced by others!
Now consider these statements:

- All husbands should support their wives financially.
- Women are much better at housework.
- Men are just as good at raising children as women.
- If a man does the cooking he is 'henpecked'.
- It is only women who really want to get married.
- People should only get married if they are in love.
- In marriage the wife must obey the husband.

As a class, discuss what kind of attitude some of those statements represent.

Introduction

The Taming of the Shrew reflects some of the attitudes towards marriage in Shakespeare's time, particularly what people regarded as the role of a man and a woman in a marriage. Parents arranged most marriages in those days.

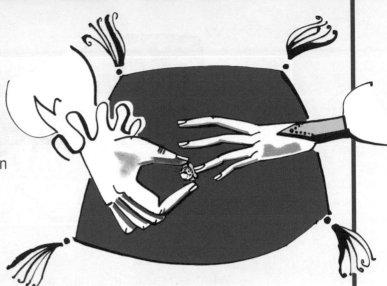

Development

DRAMA   SPEAKING AND LISTENING   READING   WRITING

1 In pairs, list the reasons why people get married.

2 In the extract below, Petruchio and his servant Grumio visit their friend Hortensio where they discuss a potential marriage.

PETRUCHIO: [...] I have thrust myself into this maze,
Haply to wive and thrive as best I may [...]

HORTENSIO: Petruchio, shall I then [...]
Wish thee to a shrewd, ill-favour'd wife?
Thou'dst thank me but a little for my counsel,
And yet I'll promise thee she shall be rich [...]

PETRUCHIO: [...] I come to wive it wealthily in Padua;
If wealthily, then happily [...]

GRUMIO: [...] he tells you flatly what his mind is. Why, give him gold enough and marry him to a puppet or [...] an old trot with ne'er a tooth in her head [...] Why, nothing comes amiss, so money comes withal.

HORTENSIO: [...] Her only fault [...]
Is that she is intolerable curst,
And shrewd, and froward, so beyond all measure [...]

PETRUCHIO: Hortensio, peace. Thou know'st not gold's effect.

HORTENSIO: Her name is Katherina Minola,
Renown'd in Padua for her scolding tongue.

[Act 1, scene 2, lines 52–98]

- In pairs discuss:
  - What is Petruchio's main motive for marriage? Find quotes as evidence.
  - Compare this to the list you made earlier. What attitude to marriage does it reveal?
- Put your list into a rank order, putting what you think are the most important reasons for marriage at the top and the least important at the end.
  - Where would Petruchio's reasons come in your rank order?
  - How are our feelings about marriage different from those of people in Shakespeare's day?

3 The following extract is from Jane Austen's *Pride and Prejudice*, first published in 1813. Charlotte is to be married to the pompous and shallow Mr Collins, despite her best friend's warnings.

'The boys were relieved from their apprehension of Charlotte's dying an old maid. [...] Mr Collins, to be sure, was neither sensible nor agreeable [...] But still he would be her husband [...] marriage had always been her object: it was the only honourable provision for well-educated young women of small fortune, and, however uncertain of giving happiness, must be their pleasantest preservative from want.'

As a class, discuss this female perspective on marriage in the early nineteenth century:

- What similarities are there with *The Taming of the Shrew*?
- How is Charlotte's position different from Petruchio's?
- Do you have more sympathy for Charlotte or Petruchio? Why?

4 Petruchio, having successfully married Katherina, is determined to 'tame' her wild, aggressive nature by bullying her as she used to do to others.

PETRUCHIO: Good Lord, how brightly and goodly shines the moon!
KATHERINA: The moon? The sun! It is not moonlight now.
PETRUCHIO: I say it is the moon that shines so bright.
KATHERINA: I know it is the sun that shines so bright.
PETRUCHIO: [...] It shall be moon, or star, or what I list,
Or e're I journey to your father's house [...]
KATHERINA: Forward, I pray, since we have come so far,
And be it moon, or sun, or what you please [...]
PETRUCHIO: I say it is the moon.
KATHERINA: I know it is the moon.
PETRUCHIO: Nay, then you lie; it is the blessed sun.
KATHERINA: [...] What you will have it nam'd, even that it is,
And so it shall be so for Katherine.

[Act 4, scene 5, lines 2–22]

With a partner, take a part each and rehearse an edited version of the extract:

● Show the different **status** of the two characters.

● Put across how Katherina is gradually changed by Petruchio's behaviour.

Review

Perform your sketches.

As a class, discuss what point you think Shakespeare may have been making about marriage in his time.

The Taming of the Shrew

WOMEN'S RIGHTS AND WRONGS

Aims

● To examine how the play reflects the attitudes towards women in its time.

Starter session

In a group, read the following statements and give a mark out of five to each one according to how true you think it is:

5 = totally true
1 = completely untrue

'Only women cry'　　'It's a man's job to be strong'

'Women are stronger than men'　　'Men must be successful'

'It's all right for men to show their emotions'　　'Men and women are equal'

'Married women should stay at home and be good housewives'

'It's right that women are beginning to get more respect in society'

'Women must be gentle and courteous at all times'

● In pairs, divide the statements above into the attitudes that you think are modern and those that are old fashioned.
● What differences do you notice?
● Feed back your results to the class.

Introduction

When Shakespeare was writing in the early seventeenth century, there existed strict divisions between the way men and women were allowed to behave. There were significant differences in their roles, for example in marriage, where traditionally the wife played the role of mother and was meant to obey her husband, and the husband was the head of the household.

Development

A DRAMA **SPEAKING AND LISTENING** **READING** **WRITING**

In the beginning of *The Taming of the Shrew* it is clear that what the male characters desire in women is in their behaviour. The men are attracted to the younger Bianca, but are terrified by her bad-tempered, aggressive sister, Katherina.

> BAPTISTA: I firmly am resolv'd [...]
> Not to bestow my youngest daughter
> Before I have a husband for the elder.
> GREMIO: [...] She's too rough for me.
> HORTENSIO: [*To Katherina*] [...] No mates for you,
> Unless you were of gentler, milder mould [...]
> From all such devils, good Lord deliver us!
> TRANIO: That wench is stark mad or wonderful froward.
> LUCENTIO: [*Looking at Bianca*] But in the other's silence do I see
> Maid's mild behaviour and sobriety.
> BIANCA: [*To Baptista, her father*] Sir, to your pleasure humbly I subscribe.
> My books and instruments shall be my company.
>
> [Act 1, scene 1, lines 49–82]

1 In groups, discuss the following points that you have learned from reading the extract:
   - Why do you think Baptista wants Katherina married before Bianca?
   - How does Katherina behave, according to the men, that is unappealing to them?
   - In contrast, what features make Bianca the perfect woman?

2 Use the title: 'The Perfect Woman?'.
   - Draw a quick sketch of Bianca, and around her label all the things that make her preferable to Katherina as far as the men are concerned.

1 A key theme in the play is the role of a husband and wife. In pairs, make a list of ingredients for the ideal husband and ideal wife.

2 Read Katherina's final speech in the play where she describes a perfect wife.

> KATHERINA: Thy husband is thy lord, thy life, thy keeper,
> Thy head, thy sovereign; one that cares for thee,
> And for thy maintenance; commits his body
> To painful labour [...]
> Whilst thou liest warm at home, secure and safe;
> And craves no other tribute at thy hands
> But love, fair looks, and true obedience;
> Too little payment for so great a debt.
> [...] place your hand below your husband's foot [...]
>
> *[Act 5, scene 2, lines 47–77]*

● In pairs, discuss how Katherina's version of the perfect wife fits in with the list you made. Do you agree with her views?

Review

As a class, discuss whether you think Shakespeare intended Katherina's final speech to be taken entirely at face value. Why else might he have used the speech?

How might a male audience in Shakespeare's time have reacted to Katherina's speech?

Homework

Write a response to Katherina's final speech outlining your views on attitudes to women. You might include:

● your reaction to the speech
● how things have changed
● the danger of accepting the seventeenth-century views.

The Taming of the Shrew

STATUS

Aims

- To look at ways in which Shakespeare establishes the **status** of characters.
- To use drama to explore issues of status.

Starter session

As a group, read the list of types of people below. Rank them according to their **external status** in our society. Put the highest at the top and least important at the bottom, although some may also have an equal status:

butcher	lawyer	pop star	millionaire	homeless person
banker	premier league footballer	government minister	teacher
plastic surgeon	scientist	postal worker	premier league footballer

- Discuss what type of person society values the most, and what it values the least according to your rank order.
- What do you think might be the difference between **internal** and **external status**? What other factors might influence someone's status apart from their job?

Introduction

In Shakespeare's day there were huge and obvious divisions between the classes in his society.

The upper class included royalty and people with titles (lords, dukes, and so on). The middle class was made up of those who had businesses or were connected to the Church. The lower class were peasants, common labourers, and the poverty stricken.

Shakespeare divided his characters into the **high** and **low characters** (characters with a higher or lower status). This was not only obvious in who they were but also in the way that they spoke.

Development

A **DRAMA** **SPEAKING AND LISTENING** ~~READING~~ ~~WRITING~~

In the beginning of *The Taming of the Shrew*, Christopher Sly, a tinker (low status) wakes from a drunken sleep and is tricked by a lord (high status) into believing that his whole life as a drunken tinker has been a dream, and that he is actually a lord himself.

[Bedchamber in the Lord's house. Sly awakes.]

2 SERVINGMAN: Will't please your honour taste of these conserves? [...]

SLY: I am Christophero Sly, call not me 'honour' nor 'lordship'. I ne'er drank sack in my life [...]

LORD: Heaven cease this idle humour in your honour!
O, that a mighty man of such descent,
Of such possessions, and so high esteem,
Should be infused with so foul a spirit!

SLY: What, would you make me mad? Am not I Christopher Sly, old Sly's son of Burton-heath, by birth a pedlar [...] and now by present profession a tinker?

LORD: [...] O noble lord, bethink thee of thy birth, [...]
Look how thy servants do attend on thee [...]
Wilt thou have music? Hark! Apollo plays, [*Music*]
And twenty caged nightingales do sing.

[Ind. 2, lines 2–34]

1 In pairs, discuss how the language of the lord and Sly reflects their status.

● What type of words does the lord use?
● Is there a difference in their style of speech?

2 With a partner, **improvise** a scene showing the different external status of two characters through their speech and behaviour. Use one of the following:

● businessman and beggar
● sergeant-major and private.

1 The internal status of a character is equally important because it is about his or her *inner strengths or weaknesses*.

For instance you may have two kings (high external status), but one king is a coward and lacks confidence (low internal status) while the other is brave and well respected (high internal status).

The following extract shows Baptista protecting Bianca from Katherina, his elder daughter:

> BAPTISTA: [*To Katherina*] When did she cross thee with a bitter word?
> KATHERINA: [...] I'll be reveng'd [*Flies after Bianca*]
> BAPTISTA: What, in my sight? [...]
> KATHERINA: [...] Now I see
> She is your treasure, she must have a husband,
> [...] Talk not to me [...]
> Till I can find occasion of revenge.
>
> *[Act 2, scene 1, lines 27–35]*

- In a group, consider what external status a father and daughter would have.
- How has Katherina's internal status changed this?

2 Rewrite this extract using a modern setting and family. How would you switch the status expectations and show the internal status of the characters?

Review

Perform your scene for the class.
As a class, discuss how drama benefits from issues of status.

Romeo and Juliet

A LOVE STORY

Aims

- To explore the conventions of Elizabethan romance.
- To examine the style of language used in a romance.

Starter session

As a group, brainstorm the idea of love and any other emotions associated with it. First, draw a big red heart in the middle of a large sheet of sugar paper. Look at your poster. Is love always an entirely positive experience?

Now, in pairs, write a recipe for 'The Perfect Romance' using at least eight ingredients that are suitable, for example 'Six tablespoons of passion, an ounce of hope, a single kiss', and so on. What does your recipe tell you about the essential elements needed for a romantic relationship to work?

Introduction

In Shakespeare's day there were rules and conventions that governed who you could have a relationship with and when a courting couple could meet (usually at closely watched formal occasions, like dances and banquets). Most relationships and marriages were arranged by the parents, regardless of whether the couple actually loved one another.

Romeo and Juliet both rebel against these 'rules'. They are determined to be together against the wishes of their families. The Elizabethans, despite all their restrictions on relationships, treasured the idea of this kind of true love. Shakespeare made the language that Romeo and Juliet use with each other reflect the ideal romantic love.

Development

1 Imagine you are Shakespeare: write the first six lines that Romeo speaks to himself when he sees Juliet for the first time. What is he thinking and feeling? What is his impression of her?

- Look at your six lines: what words, phrase or images did you use to show his feelings?

2 Read the extract below where Romeo has gatecrashed the Capulets' party and sees Juliet on the dance floor.

ROMEO: O, she doth teach the torches to burn bright.
It seems she hangs upon the cheek of night
As a rich jewel in an Ethiop's ear –
Beauty too rich for use, for earth too dear,
So shows a snowy dove trooping with crows
As yonder lady o'er her fellows shows.
[…] I ne'er saw true beauty till this night.

[Act 1, scene 5, lines 43–51]

- In pairs, consider how Shakespeare has shown Romeo's feelings in the way he has used language:
  - Why does it resemble poetry?
  - What poetic techniques has he used?
  - Why does he use the images of 'torches', 'a rich jewel' and 'a snowy dove'? What are these things associated with?
- Are there any sounds that are particularly used? Why those sounds?
- Are there any similarities between Shakespeare's approach, ideas and images, and those you used earlier?

- In your pair, invent the worst chat-up lines possible. Make them truly revolting and guaranteed to put anyone off! Then read the extract below from the famous balcony scene where Romeo makes clear his feelings for Juliet. Compare it with your chat-up lines.

ROMEO:
$$\overset{x}{} \overset{/}{} \quad \overset{x}{} \quad \overset{/}{} \quad \overset{x}{} \quad \overset{/}{} \overset{x}{} \quad \overset{/}{} \overset{x}{} \quad \overset{/}{}$$
But soft! What light through yonder window breaks?
It is the east and Juliet is the sun!
Arise fair sun, and kill the envious moon
Who is already sick and pale with grief
That thou her maid art far more fair than she.

[Act 2, scene 2, lines 2–6]

x = *unstressed syllable*   / = *stressed syllable*

- Quickly translate Romeo's speech into modern English.
- Compare the style of your translation with that of the speech. Which is more appealing? Why?
- What do you notice about the rhythm of the first line? Why has Shakespeare given it a rhythm?
- Find another line with the same rhythm.

Review

As a class, discuss what aspects of style the Elizabethans favoured for the language of romance.

Would Romeo's lines actually work in real life?

Homework
Write the next ten lines to Romeo's speech. The first line is:
'It is my lady, O it is my love!'

Use those aspects of Shakespeare's style that you explored today.

Romeo and Juliet

A STORY OF HATRED

Aims

● To explore the theme of conflict and rivalry through drama.

Starter session

Two rival families, the Capulets and Montagues, set the background for *Romeo and Juliet*. Both families are powerful, rich, proud and influential.

Your teacher will divide the class in half: one group will be the Capulets and the other the Montagues.

● Both groups are to make a **still life** formal portrait of their family.
● The families should include the following characters:

Capulets	Montagues
Lord and Lady Capulet	Lord and Lady Montague
Juliet	Romeo
Tybalt (Juliet's cousin)	Benvolio (Romeo's friend)
Juliet's Nurse	Servants, guards, etc.
Servants, guards, etc.	

● Make the different characters clear by focusing on where they are positioned and showing their status.
● Present your family portraits.

As a class, discuss how the other group showed the differences in status. What qualities or characteristics did they give their family?

Introduction

Romeo and Juliet is famous as a love story, but it is equally a story about hatred. It is the warring between the Capulets and Montagues resulting from 'an ancient grudge' that eventually tears the lovers apart and brings about the play's tragic end.

The very opening scene involves a dramatic street fight between groups from the two opposing families.

Development

DRAMA   SPEAKING AND LISTENING   READING   WRITING

Read this extract where Sampson and Gregory, servants of the Capulet household, encounter Abram and Balthasar, the Montagues' servants, in a public place. This exchange takes place just before they start to fight:

GREGORY: I will frown as I pass by, and let them take it as they list.

SAMPSON: [...] I will bite my thumb at them, which is disgrace to them if they bear it.

ABRAM: Do you bite your thumb at us, sir?

SAMPSON: I do bite my thumb, sir.

ABRAM: Do you bite your thumb at us, sir?

SAMPSON: Is the law of our side if I say ay?

GREGORY: No.

SAMPSON: No sir, I do not bite my thumb at you, sir, but I bite my thumb, sir.

GREGORY: Do you quarrel, sir?

ABRAM: Quarrel, sir? No, sir.

SAMPSON: But if you do, sir, I am for you. I serve as good a man as you.

[Act 1, scene 1, lines 41–52]

1 In pairs, discuss:

● What are Sampson and Gregory trying to do to the Montagues by frowning and thumb-biting at them?
● What is the difference between what Sampson and Abram say, and what they actually mean in these two lines?

SAMPSON: No, sir, I do not bite my thumb at you, sir [...]
ABRAM: Quarrel, sir? No, sir.

● Why don't they say what they mean? Are they being genuinely polite?

2 In pairs, role-play Sampson and Abram facing-off before the fight. You have to provoke the other into making the first move *without* making obvious threats or insults.

3 Read what happens immediately after the extract above. Benvolio, a

Rules

◆ No physical contact.

◆ Don't be too obvious – you don't have to say what you really mean. For example, you could say 'Are you looking at me?' instead of 'Don't look at me! You wanna fight?!'

◆ *How* you say your lines will be important.

Montague, and the Capulet, Tybalt, have entered:

● In pairs, discuss what we learn about Benvolio and Tybalt's

SAMPSON: Draw if you be men. [*They fight.*]
BENVOLIO: Part, fools, [*Beats down their swords*]
        [...] you know not what you do.
  TYBALT: [...] Turn thee, Benvolio, look upon thy death.
BENVOLIO: I do but keep the peace [...]
  TYBALT: What, drawn, and talk of peace? I hate the word,
        As I hate hell, all Montagues, and thee.

[*Act 1, scene 1, lines 60–9*]

characters and their attitude to the fight.

● In pairs, improvise one person playing Tybalt and the other Benvolio. Tybalt must try to provoke Benvolio into the fight but Benvolio must find reasons to resist.

● Swap your roles over and repeat the improvisation.

Review

Present a short extract from your last role-play.
As a class, discuss how Shakespeare makes the opening of the play exciting.

Romeo and Juliet

THE LOVERS

Aims

- To study the character differences between Romeo and Juliet.

Starter session

To gain insight into the differences between Romeo and Juliet you should first consider how boys and girls think and behave differently.

- As a group, discuss what are the typical things that boys and girls say.
- On a large piece of paper, make two columns. On one side draw the outline of a girl's head and on the other side the outline of a boy's head. Fill each of the heads with the typical thoughts of a boy or girl. For example:

BOYS
- 'Manchester United are the best'
- 'Girls are so strange'
- 'I need FOOD!'

GIRLS
- 'Boys are so immature'
- 'I need some new face cream'
- 'Boys! Boys! Boys!'

- As a class, discuss whether these are accurate portrayals of what boys and girls are really like. What seem to be the essential differences?

Introduction

Romeo and Juliet was written at a time when people married at a very early age by today's standards. Both Romeo and Juliet are only teenagers. Lord Capulet tells Paris that his daughter 'hath not seen the change of fourteen years' [*Act 1, scene 2, line 9*].

Readers sometimes make the mistake of thinking that both the main characters are identical. Shakespeare has, however, made clear distinctions between their personalities and the way they behave and speak.

Development

A DRAMA   **SPEAKING AND LISTENING**   **READING**   WRITING

Read this extract from the famous 'balcony scene', where Romeo, a Montague, has dared to creep into the Capulets' grounds in the hope of seeing Juliet.

JULIET: How cam'st thou hither, tell me [...]
         The orchard walls are high and hard to climb,
         And the place death, considering who thou art,
         If any of my kinsmen find thee here.
ROMEO: With love's light wings did I o'erperch these walls,
         For stony limits cannot hold love out, [...]
         Therefore thy kinsmen are no stop to me. [...]
JULIET: Dost thou love me? I know thou wilt say 'Ay',
         And I will take thy word. Yet, if thou swear'st,
         Thou mayst prove false [...]
         Although I joy in thee,
         I have no joy of this contract tonight:
         It is too rash, too unadvis'd, too sudden [...]
ROMEO: O wilt thou leave me so unsatisfied?
JULIET: What satisfaction canst thou have tonight?
ROMEO: Th'exchange of thy love's faithful vow for mine.
JULIET: I gave thee mine before thou didst request it [...]

[Act 2, scene 2, lines 62–128]

1 In pairs, discuss:

- What do you notice about the style of Romeo's first speech?
- How does Juliet react to Romeo's presence and declarations of love?
- Does Romeo respond to Juliet's concerns?
- Who is more realistic? Who seems to be more mature?

Romeo is banished for the death of Tybalt and Juliet is forced to marry Paris. Read their reactions to the news.

EXTRACT A

NURSE: [*To Romeo*] Blubbering and weeping [...]
Stand up [...] Stand, and you be a man,
For Juliet's sake [...]

[*Romeo draws his sword to kill himself*]
FRIAR LAURENCE: Hold thy desperate hand.
[...] Thy Juliet is alive [...]

[Act 3, scene 3, lines 86–135]

EXTRACT B

FRIAR LAURENCE: O Juliet, I already know thy grief [...]
JULIET: Tell me not, Friar [...]
Unless thou tell me how I may prevent it [...]
Give me some present counsel, or behold:
[...] this bloody knife
Shall play the umpire [...]
I long to die,
If what thou speak'st speak not of remedy.
FRIAR LAURENCE: Hold, daughter; I do spy a kind of hope [...]

[Act 4, scene 1, lines 46–68]

2 Divide your page into two columns, one headed Romeo and the other Juliet. Note down in the appropriate column how they react to their circumstances and what this tells us about their characters. Add any other information you have learned about them.

Review

As a class, discuss what you have discovered to be the differences between Romeo and Juliet. How do they compare with the characteristics of boys and girls identified in the Starter session?

Homework

Write a brief report on how far you think Romeo and Juliet fit the stereotypes of boys and girls.

Romeo and Juliet

TRAGEDY AND FATE

Aims

● To study how key themes are developed through the structure of the play.

Starter session

You may love horoscopes or loathe them, but still find them fascinating, as they supposedly offer you a glimpse of your future according to your star sign. If Romeo and Juliet had been able to look into the future, would they have acted differently?

● In pairs, conduct a quick survey of the class to see who reads horoscopes and who believes in them.

● In groups, you are going to carry out an experiment to test the accuracy of horoscopes.

Read the two examples of character types according to their star-signs (the actual star-signs have been removed*):

1 'You're an artistic, dreamy, warm character. You're easygoing, trusting and can sometimes be too laid-back. Don't let people take advantage of you; you must be more assertive!'

2 'You have a sharp, ambitious personality and you love a challenge with your boundless energy. Your endless enthusiasm shows an adventurous love of life!'

● See how many people in your class fit these personality types; write their names down.

● Next, ask each of those people what their star sign is. Are they all the same star sign? What does this tell you about how accurate the star sign personalities were?

(*answers at the end of this unit on page 66)

Introduction

The Prologue refers to Romeo and Juliet as 'star-cross'd lovers', meaning that their lives were influenced by the movement and position of the stars. This idea was known as 'predetermination' or, more commonly, 'Fate'. In Medieval times many philosophers believed that people's lives had already been mapped out for them, from birth until death, because of the influence of the stars. According to this thinking, the tragic deaths of Romeo and Juliet were unavoidable. They were powerless to do anything as their fate had already been decided.

Development

DRAMA   **SPEAKING AND LISTENING**   **READING**   **WRITING**

The Prologue tells the entire story of *Romeo and Juliet* so the audience knows from the beginning how the play will end. The Prologue almost acts like Fate itself, as it says exactly what will happen to the lovers.

1 In pairs, pick out the words and phrases, which you think refer to the idea of Fate. How often does this idea occur in the passage?

THE PROLOGUE

[Enter Chorus]
Two households both alike in dignity
(In fair Verona, where we lay our scene)
From ancient grudge break to new mutiny,
Where civil blood makes civil hands unclean.
From forth the fatal loins of these two foes
A pair of star-cross'd lovers take their life,
Whose misadventur'd piteous overthrows
Doth with their death bury their parents' strife.
The fearful passage of their death-mark'd love
And the continuance of their parents' rage,
Which, but their children's end, nought could remove,
Is now the two hours' traffic of our stage.

2 In a group, act out the entire story of *Romeo and Juliet* in three minutes, as told in the Prologue.

- Someone must be the narrator reading the Prologue.
- The actors' actions must follow what is being read.
- Consider how the recurring idea of Fate can be put across dramatically.

3 The way in which the play develops is vital, as it unfolds what the audience knows will be the inevitable tragedy. Below is a list of some of the key moments in the play that contribute to the tragic ending.

Friar Laurence decides to marry Romeo and Juliet.

Capulets and Montagues fight in public.

Romeo is persuaded to gate crash the Capulet ball.

The letter about Juliet's fake death fails to reach Romeo.

Juliet fakes her own death.

Romeo kills himself just before Juliet wakes.

Capulet forces Juliet to marry Paris.

Tybalt slays Mercutio; Romeo kills Tybalt.

- Put these events on a time-line according to the order they come in the play.

Prologue ├───┤ End

- In a group, discuss which event(s) you think had the most influence on the tragic ending? Are there any obvious choices?

4 Understanding the idea of Fate and knowing how the play ends often gives a greater significance to what characters say. Read the extracts on the next page.

[During Romeo and Juliet's wedding night]

JULIET: O God, I have an ill-divining soul!
Methinks I see thee, now thou art so low,
As one dead in the bottom of a tomb.

[Act 3, scene 5, lines 54–6]

[After Romeo is banished from Verona]

ROMEO: I dreamt my lady came and found me dead [...]
And breath'd such life with kisses in my lips
That I reviv'd [...]

[Act 5, scene 1, lines 6–8]

- In pairs, discuss what both these premonitions are about?
  – In what way do they come true in the end?
  – Why has Shakespeare included them? What effect does it have on the audience?

5 Now, write a horoscope prediction for the characters of Romeo, Juliet and Tybalt. Use the example below, for Friar Laurence, as a model.

Your STARS this week!

You Librans just love to control things, but BEWARE! Things are not always as they seem – tread cautiously. Someone close to you may be making rash decisions, but keep a level head and be prepared to deal with a major crisis.

Review

Read aloud your horoscope predictions.
As a class, discuss why the idea of Fate makes the play tragic?

(Horoscope answers: 1 Pisces; 2 Aries)

Romeo and Juliet

BAPTISTA AND CAPULET: BAD FATHERS?

Aims

- To study the theme of parents.
- To compare two characters from different plays.

Starter session

- Make a list of qualities for the 'perfect parent'.
- Compare your list with a partner. What are the similarities or differences?
- Make a list of characteristics for 'real parents' next to your 'perfect parent' list.

Perfect parent	Real parent
Always happy	Sometimes gets cross
Really trendy	Terrible shoes!

- As a class, discuss what things parents decide for you. Do they have the right to make these decisions for you?

Introduction

The role of fathers is important in Shakespeare's plays. You will be comparing Baptista Minola (*The Taming of the Shrew*) and Lord Capulet (*Romeo and Juliet*) by assessing their similarities and differences. The lives of their daughters, Katherina and Juliet, depend on their decisions and actions.

Your assessment will take the form of a competition to see who gains the most points.

Development

Round 1: dealing with suitors

Read these extracts:

> PARIS: But now my lord, what say you to my suit?
> CAPULET: [...] My child is yet a stranger in the world,
>   She hath not seen the change of fourteen years.
>   Let two more summers wither in their pride
>   Ere we may think her ripe to be a bride.
>   [...] She is the hopeful lady of my earth.
>   But woo her, gentle Paris, get her heart [...]
>
> *[Act 1, scene 2, lines 6–16]*

> PETRUCHIO: Pray, have you not a daughter
>   Call'd Katherina, fair and virtuous?
> BAPTISTA: I have a daughter, sir, call'd Katherina.
> PETRUCHIO: I am a gentleman of Verona, sir,
>   That hearing of her beauty and her wit,
>   [...] Am bold to show myself a forward guest [...]
> BAPTISTA: Y'are welcome, sir [...]
>   But for my daughter Katherine [...]
>   She is not for your turn, the more my grief [...]
> PETRUCHIO: [...] Then tell me if I get your daughter's love,
>   What dowry shall I have [...]?
> BAPTISTA: [...] The one half of my lands
>   And [...] twenty thousand crowns
>   [...] when the special thing is well obtain'd
>   That is, her love; for that is all in all.
>
> *[Act 2, scene 1, lines 42–128]*

In pairs, discuss:

● How do Capulet's references to Juliet differ from the way Baptista speaks about Katherina?

● How do they differ in responding to their daughters' suitors?

● In the final line of both speeches, what do they insist the suitors must do?

● Give Baptista and Capulet a mark out of five for how they regard their daughters: 5 = highest; 1 = lowest.

● Write three bullet points for each character giving a reason for your mark.

Round 2: dealing with crisis

The following section focuses on how the two fathers deal with their daughters in a crisis.

[After Tybalt's death, Capulet arranges for Juliet to marry Paris as quickly as possible.]

CAPULET: [*To Juliet*] Fettle your fine joints 'gainst Thursday next
To go with Paris to Saint Peter's Church,
Or I will drag thee on a hurdle thither.
[…] Hang thee young baggage, disobedient wretch!

[Act 3, scene 5, lines 153–60]

[On Katherina's wedding day Petruchio, the groom, leaves the guests waiting. Katherina leaves, crying.]

BAPTISTA: I cannot blame thee now to weep, For such an injury would
vex a saint […]

[Eventually Petruchio arrives, but in an outrageous outfit.]

BAPTISTA: Why, sir, you know this is your wedding-day. […]
Fie, doff this habit […]
An eyesore to our solemn festival!

[Act 3, scene 2, lines 27–28, 93–97]

- In pairs, discuss which father takes into account his daughter's feelings? How do they differ in the way they deal with their daughters?
- Give each a mark out of five including bullet points for reasons.

Round 3: the consequences

- In groups, consider the ending of both plays: which father's actions has more disastrous consequences?
- Give each a mark out of five including bullet points for reasons.

Review

Tell the class the total points you gave to each character. What are their similarities and differences?

Homework

Rewrite one of the situations in the extracts from this unit in the style of a modern soap opera.

Writing about Shakespeare's plays

Aims

- To be able to refine your ideas about the plays you have studied.
- To write a comparison of two characters.

Starter session

To write a formal essay where you are required to make comparisons you must use a formal style. This will involve the use of **connectives**.

Connectives are words or phrases that link clauses, sentences and paragraphs. Read the passage below.

Since his death, many have proclaimed Shakespeare the best playwright in the English language. Although this is an ambitious claim he is undeniably the most famous.

Despite the fact that reading is no longer as popular a pastime most of the population of this country have read at least one of Shakespeare's plays. Indeed, we often recognise his verse instantly. For instance, who hasn't heard the lines 'To be, or not to be' or 'Romeo, Romeo, wherefore art thou Romeo'?

However, there are those that believe Shakespeare did not write the plays. Moreover, some scholars have found evidence that it may have actually been a playwright called Christopher Marlowe who was responsible for the fine works we have come to admire as Shakespeare's.

Despite these claims, no conclusive evidence has yet been found. Perhaps we feel more comfortable believing in the myth of Shakespeare.

- In pairs, identify connectives used in the passage.
- Connectives serve various purposes. Make a list of connectives that might be used to contrast and compare ideas, for example *on the other hand, similarly*.

Introduction

You will be writing a 500 word essay entitled 'A comparison of two Shakespearean fathers: Baptista Minola and Lord Capulet'.

In this essay you will use the knowledge you have gained of *Romeo and Juliet* and *The Taming of the Shrew* to compare and contrast the two characters.

You should refer to the previous lesson to gather the evidence you will need.

Development

DRAMA   **SPEAKING AND LISTENING**   READING   **WRITING**

1 In pairs:

- Brainstorm what you remember of the characters of Baptista and Capulet.
- Include their actions, behaviour and attitudes towards their daughters.
- Do this on two separate sheets, one for each character.
- Find some short quotes to back up your points.

2 Using your notes, make a comparison/contrast sheet for the two characters under the following headings:

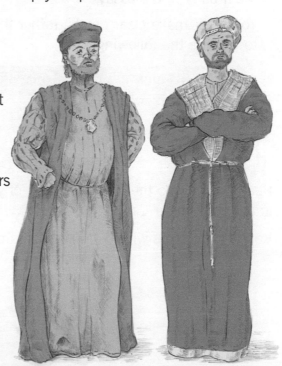

- Attitude towards daughters at the beginning of the plays
- Reasons for wanting daughters married
- How they treat their daughters
- The final consequences of what they do.

These headings will eventually help you structure your essay into four distinct parts.

3 Begin writing the introduction for your essay.

You must:

- Make clear the purpose of the essay.
- Provide basic, factual information about Baptista and Capulet (without going into too much depth) and their role in the plays.
- Briefly outline of the plot of both plays.

4a You must use the appropriate connectives to compare and contrast the characters (refer to your Starter session activity for help).

Practise using connectives in the following exercise by joining and rewriting the following sentences:

Baptista is at a loss. He doesn't know what to do. His daughter's behaviour troubles him. She is wild and unruly. He comes up with a solution.

Capulet is different. He thinks Juliet is too young to be married. Paris asks for her hand in marriage. Capulet wants him to wait.

4b Which of the following could you use as a connective at the start of the second paragraph?

Maybe   However   Because   In contrast   Later

5 Use the four headings you were given in question 2 to structure the main body of the essay.

You must make clear points, rather than retelling the story. Remember to provide the following:

P = Point   E = Explanation   E = Evidence

Review

Read out loud to the class a section of your essay that makes a clear point about Baptista or Capulet.

Read an example where you've used a connective.

Henry V

A CHRISTIAN KING

Aims

- To explore the complexities of the character of Henry as the king.
- To study the dramatic impact of a scene.
- To look at interpretations of the King in different media.

Starter session

Below are pictures from two famous film versions of *Henry V* (Kenneth Branagh, 1989, and Laurence Olivier, 1944).

- In a small group, brainstorm the different aspects of the king each of the actors was attempting to put across in the pictures. How do the two versions differ from each other?
- Now, working in pairs, read the dauphin (prince) of France's thoughts about the English king's reputation:

> DAUPHIN: For, my good leige, she [England] is so idly kinged,
> Her sceptre so fantastically borne
> By a vain, giddy, shallow, humorous youth [...]
>
> [Act 2, scene 4, lines 26–28]

- What kind of king do the French believe King Henry to be? How does the Dauphin talk about him?
- How does this view of the king compare with the pictures you have looked at?

Introduction

Henry V tells the story of Prince Hal's rise as king of England after a wayward youth spent neglecting royal duties and mixing with drunkards and outlaws. As King, Hal has to prove his worth and lead his country against the French enemy in the face of his disreputable youth.

Development

Read the following extract where the king makes clear to the lords his claims over France.

> KING: Now are we well resolved; and by God's help
> And yours, the noble sinews of our power,
> France being ours, we'll bend it to our awe,
> Or break it all to pieces. Or there we'll sit,
> Ruling in large and ample empery
> O'er France and all her almost kingly dukedoms,
> Or lay these bones in an unworthy urn,
> Tombless, with no remembrance over them.
>
> [Act 1, scene 2, lines 222–229]

1 With a partner, discuss the following points:

  ● How might you describe the king's attitude towards France?
  ● Look at the last two lines. What is at stake for the king here?

2 In a group of four create a still life of the scene above.

  ● How will you convey King Henry's higher status over the other noblemen?
  ● How can you put across his determination?
  ● How will the others react to his plan?
  ● Once you have tried a still life, attempt an improvisation of the extract above with about four lines being spoken.

3 With your group, discuss how this picture of the king compares with the dauphin's view of him as seen in the Starter session.

  ● Create an alternative still life that reflects the French view of Henry as king. How will you change his status and character?

4 Imagine you are the play's director. Prepare the actors' notes on the following extract. Focus on these areas:

  ● how to speak the lines (tone of voice and emotion)
  ● what movements or gestures could be used
  ● the reactions and facial expressions that could be used.

Here the dauphin mocks King Henry by having the French ambassador present him with the insultingly worthless 'gift' of tennis balls in response to his demands for certain lands (dukedoms) in France.

AMBASSADOR: He therefore sends you, [...]
This tun of treasure, and in lieu of this
Desires you let the dukedoms that you claim [...]

KING: What treasure, uncle?

EXETER: Tennis-balls, my liege.

KING: We are glad the Dauphin is so pleasant with us; [...]
When we have matched our rackets to these balls
We will in France, by God's grace, play a set
Shall strike his father's crown into the hazard. [...]
And tell the pleasant Prince this mock of his
Hath turned his balls to gun-stones, and his soul
Shall stand sore charged for the wasteful vengeance
That shall fly with them.

[Act 1, scene 2, lines 254–84]

● In a group, compare your notes and rehearse a short performance of the scene. Don't use the full script, but just include key lines.

Review

Take turns to show examples of your performances.
As a class, consider what makes King Henry a dramatic character.

Henry V

A MUSE OF FIRE

Aims

- To explore the different attitudes towards war in Henry V.
- To compare *Henry V*'s portrayal of war with that of a First World War poet.
- To understand the importance of literary texts over time.

Starter session

War is something that has been with humankind since the beginning of civilisation, although attitudes to war have varied through the ages.

You are going to conduct a short experiment to find out the class' views of war.

- Begin by brainstorming 'WAR'. You have three minutes to do this.
- Don't show your results to anyone else! When your time is up, divide the things on your list into three categories:

1 Positive (e.g. victory)	2 Negative (e.g. destruction)	3 Neutral (e.g. soldiers, guns, etc.)

- Total up your scores for each category. Which one has the most on your list?
- As a class, compare your scores. In which category did people score the most? Were people's results more or less the same?
- Discuss what these class findings tell you about people's attitudes to war today. Do you think the results might have been different if this experiment had been conducted a hundred years ago? Give reasons for your answers.

Introduction

Henry V is a play about war, but Shakespeare doesn't present us with any single idea. Instead, he shows us contrasting views and allows the audience to decide which they agree with.

Development

A | **DRAMA** | **SPEAKING AND LISTENING** | **READING** | **WRITING**

King Henry faces seemingly insurmountable odds before the battle of Agincourt: his men are weary, hugely outnumbered and demoralised. In the following speech, he rouses and inspires his army resulting in their victory over the French.

KING: If we are marked to die, we are enough
To do our country loss, and if to live,
The fewer men, the greater share of honour [...]
By Jove, I am not covetous for gold [...]
It earns me not if men my garments wear:
Such outward things dwell not in my desires.
But if it be a sin to covet honour
I am the most offending soul alive.
[...] He which hath no stomach to this fight,
Let him depart; his passport shall be made [...]
We would not die in that man's company
That fears his fellowship to die with us.
This day is called the feast of Crispian.
He that outlives this day and comes safe home
Will stand a-tiptoe when this day is named,
And rouse him at the name of Crispian. [...]
But he'll remember, with advantages,
What feats he did that day [...]
And Crispin Crispian shall ne'er go by
From this day to the ending of the world
But we in it shall be remembered,
We few, we happy few, we band of brothers.
For he today that sheds his blood with me
Shall be my brother. [...]

[Act 4, scene 3, lines 20–62]

1 In pairs, discuss and make a list of the techniques that King Henry uses to inspire his men.

- What is it that the king himself 'covets'?
- What does he claim they will gain by fighting?
- Comment on the last three lines. Why might this inspire his men?
- Outline the positive aspects that the king claims about war. Are these similar to the things on your 'positive' list from the Starter session activity?

2 You are going to imagine that you are the actor playing the part of the king. Consider how you will deliver an extract of the speech to your class.

- With your partner, select a short extract (roughly four or five lines), which you think is particularly persuasive.
- Rehearse with each other. Take turns to play the actor and the director.
- Remember that you are delivering your lines in a way that will inspire your men to die for you.
- Perform your extract to the class.

3 In a small group, read the poem below, which was written during the First World War, by Charles Sorley.

IN MEMORIAM S.C.W., V.C.
(8 September 1915)

There is no fitter end than this.
No need is now to yearn nor sigh.
We know the glory that is his,
A glory that can never die.

Surely we knew it long before,
Knew all along that he was made
For a swift radiant morning, for
A sacrificing swift night-shade.

In your group, discuss the following:

- The poem gives a positive view of war. Pick out the key words that reinforce this view.
- What has happened to the character in the poem? How does the poet feel about this?
- How are some of the ideas about war here similar to those in King Henry's speech?

B DRAMA   *SPEAKING AND LISTENING*   *READING*   WRITING

Read the extract below where Gower, an officer in the king's army, tells of atrocities committed during the battle of Agincourt.

GOWER: 'Tis certain there's not a boy left alive, and the cowardly rascals that ran from the battle ha' done this slaughter. Besides, they have burned and carried away all that was in the King's tent, wherefore the King most worthily hath caused every soldier to cut his prisoner's throat. O, 'tis a gallant king!

[Act 4, scene 7, lines 5–10]

1 In pairs, discuss how this view of war contrasts the 'Crispin Day' speech.
  - How is war portrayed here?
  - What do you think of the king's command in the last three lines?

2 With your partner, rehearse how an actor might deliver this speech.
  - How will the tone be different from Henry's 'Crispin Day' speech?
  - What will Gower be feeling?
  - How might he say the last three lines? Approvingly or perhaps sarcastically?

Review

As a class, discuss why the scene of the boys' massacre comes soon after the king's 'Crispin Day' speech. What might these scenes reveal about Shakespeare's views on war?

Do either of these scenes reflect your personal feelings about war?

Henry V and the power of rhetoric

Aims

- To examine the use of rhetorical devices.
- To compare Shakespeare's style with that of a twentieth-century writer.

Starter session

Read the extract below from the opening of a speech persuading pupils to take action against bullying:

> 'The situation is awful, yes, it's simply not on. I hope you think so too because we can all do something about it. You and me, together. Now I have a few suggestions, and I hope they're all right, but tell me later if they aren't. Okay, here goes; first, I think we should just tell bullies to go away and leave us alone. I mean they just cause trouble for us all, and I really don't want any more trouble...'

As a group, discuss whether the speech is effective.
- What are its weaknesses?
- Are there any strengths?

In your groups, make a list of strategies to make this speech more persuasive so that people would take action.

Introduction

Since Medieval times **rhetoric**, or the power to use language to persuade, was seen as an art – there even existed handbooks that listed **rhetorical devices**.

These rhetorical devices have been used by speech-makers, politicians and leaders through the centuries. Some well-known devices are listed below:

- addressing the audience directly
- repetition
- using **emotive language**
- **alliteration**.

Development

DRAMA **SPEAKING AND LISTENING** **READING** **WRITING**

Before the gates of the city of Harfleur the English are under heavy fire. King Henry rallies his troops for one last push to overcome the town walls and defeat the French.

HENRY: Once more unto the breach, dear friends, once more,
Or close the wall up with our English dead.
In peace there's nothing so becomes a man
As modest stillness and humility;
But when the blast of war blows in our ears,
Then imitate the action of the tiger:
Stiffen the sinews, summon up the blood,
Disguise fair nature with hard-favoured rage.
Then lend the eye a terrible aspect [...]
Now set the teeth and stretch the nostril wide,
Hold hard the breath and bend up every spirit
To his full height. On, on you noble English [...]
Be copy now to men of grosser blood
And teach them how to war [...]
The game's afoot.
Follow your spirit, and upon this charge
Cry 'God for Harry! England and Saint George!'
[King Henry and his army charge forward].

[Act 3, scene 1, lines 1–34]

1 In pairs, discuss the following points:

- What feelings do you think the king is trying to inspire in his men?
- Which lines do you think are particularly persuasive?
- What rhetorical devices does the king use to inspire his men? Use the list in the Introduction to help you.

2 Read the extract below from George Orwell's *Animal Farm*, where Old Major, the leader of the animals, gives them a speech.

'Is it not crystal clear then comrades, that all the evils of this life of ours spring from the tyranny of human beings? [...] What then must we do? Why, work night and day, body and soul, for the overthrow of the human race! That is my message to you comrades: Rebellion! [...]

And among us animals let there be perfect unity, perfect comradeship in the struggle. All men are enemies. All animals are comrades.'

- In what way is Old Major's speech similar to King Henry's?
- What rhetorical devices are used here?

3 Now rewrite the *opening paragraph* to the speech you read in the Starter session, persuading pupils to take action against bullying.

- Your audience will be your fellow students.
- Use the rhetorical devices you have seen in the two extracts.
- What emotive words or ideas could you use?

Review

Now you have attempted to write persuasively, read aloud the opening of your speech.

As a class, discuss which emotions are being appealed to in the various examples you have heard.

Homework

Write the *final paragraph* to your speech.

- What do you want the audience to feel by the end?
- What action should they take?
- How can you devise a memorable slogan for a big finish?

Macbeth

HERO OR VILLAIN?

Aims

● To study the development of a complex character through a play.

Starter session

● As a group, brainstorm what elements make a hero.
● Now in pairs, read this passage from the beginning of *Macbeth* where a soldier tells of Macbeth's battle against the rebel leader, Macdonwald.

CAPTAIN: For brave Macbeth (well he deserves that name),
Disdaining Fortune, with his brandish'd steel,
Which smok'd with bloody execution,
Like Valour's minion, carv'd out his passage,
Till he fac'd the slave;
[...] he unseam'd him from the nave to th' chops
And fix'd his head upon our battlements.

[Act 1, scene 2, lines 16–23]

● Pick out any lines or phrases that put Macbeth in a heroic light.
● What impression do we get of Macbeth at the beginning of the play?
● In a group of four, use the passage above to make three **still-life** pictures to represent front page newspaper photos of Macbeth as war hero; with each picture have a fitting headline.

Introduction

Macbeth is a **complex character**. As you have seen, he begins the play as a hero, having saved Scotland from the Scandinavian and rebel armies. But things change as the play progresses and the chance of becoming king is put in front of him. Shakespeare, however, makes it difficult for us to regard Macbeth as simply a hero or villain.

Development

A DRAMA **SPEAKING AND LISTENING** **READING** **WRITING**

When Macbeth is confronted with the opportunity to kill King Duncan and become king himself, he is faced with a moral dilemma.

- Imagine you find £50 on the pavement and there's nobody about. Put in bullet points the arguments for and against keeping the money.
- In pairs, consider how the following factors might influence you: the owner turns up clearly distressed looking for the money; the owner of the money is a bully in school.
- Read Macbeth's **soliloquy** where he weighs up the arguments for killing the king.

MACBETH: If it were done, when 'tis done, then 'twere well
It were done quickly:
[...] but this blow
Might be the be-all and the end-all here –
[...] But in these cases,
We still have judgment here; that we but teach
Bloody instructions, which, being taught, return
To plague th'inventor:
[...] He's here in double trust:
First, as I am his kinsman and his subject,
[...] then, as his host,
Who should against his murtherer shut the door,
Not bear the knife myself. Besides, this Duncan
[...] his virtues
Will plead like angels [...]

[Act 1, scene 7, lines 1–19]

- Draw up two columns on a page and, using bullet points, write down Macbeth's reasons for and against killing Duncan in the appropriate column.
- In pairs, discuss what this reveals about Macbeth's state of mind. Is he evil?

B DRAMA **SPEAKING AND LISTENING** **READING** WRITING

By the end of the play Macbeth has murdered Duncan and reigned as king using terror and brutality. But has he simply become a villain?

- Read Macbeth's soliloquy at the end when his downfall is imminent:

MACBETH: To-morrow, and to-morrow, and to-morrow,
Creeps in this petty pace from day to day,
To the last syllable of recorded time;
And all our yesterdays have lighted fools
The way to dusty death. Out, out, brief candle!
Life's but a walking shadow, a poor player,
That struts and frets his hour upon the stage,
And then is heard no more; it is a tale
Told by an idiot, full of sound and fury,
Signifying nothing.

[Act 5, scene 5, lines 19–28]

- As a group, consider how Shakespeare wanted the audience to feel about Macbeth at the end. Use the following hints to help you:
  - How does he now feel about his life (first three lines)?
  - What does it seem is the only thing he has to look forward to?
  - Find the images and phrases referring to death.
  - After this speech, do we regard Macbeth as a monster despite what he has done?

Review

As a class, discuss why we can't simply see Macbeth as a villain by the end.

What makes Macbeth a complex character?

Macbeth

THE MURDER

Aims

- To analyse the language, form and dramatic impact of a scene.

Starter session

An effective scene must be constructed with close attention to the way the characters speak and how the writer wants the audience to react to them. In pairs, read the scene below involving two murderers:

CHARLIE: Have you done it? Is he dead yet?

ED: Yeah, done it, guv.

CHARLIE: You sure?

ED: 'Course I'm sure. I done it didn't I?

CHARLIE: Why don't you just go back and check.

ED: No way! You go.

CHARLIE: What's the matter? You scared?

ED: No, I ain't scared of nothin'.

CHARLIE: You looked dead scared to me. I think you're chicken *[starts making clucking chicken sounds]*.

ED: Shut it! You're always telling me what to do!

- With a partner, act out the scene. Consider what tone the scene should have. Are there any clues to characterisation?
- As a group, discuss how effective this is as a murder scene. How might the audience respond to it? What could be changed to make it more effective?

Introduction

You will be studying Act 2, scene 2, the 'murder scene' in *Macbeth* and concentrating on how Shakespeare has constructed an emotional and dramatic scene.

Significantly, Shakespeare doesn't show us the actual murder of the king, but instead allows us to see the reaction of the murderers, Macbeth and Lady Macbeth.

Development

It is late night in Macbeth's castle. Lady Macbeth has drugged the king's servants and awaits the arrival of Macbeth who has gone to kill the king.

MACBETH: *[Within]* Who's there? – what, ho!

LADY MACBETH: Alack! I am afraid they have awak'd,
And 'tis not done.
[…] Hark! I laid their daggers ready;
He could not miss 'em. Had he not resembled
My father as he slept, I had done't. – My husband!
Enter MACBETH

MACBETH: I have done the deed. Didst thou not hear a noise?

LADY MACBETH: … Did not you speak?

MACBETH: When?

LADY MACBETH: Now.

MACBETH: As I descended?

LADY MACBETH: Ay.
[…]

MACBETH: This is a sorry sight. *[Looking on his hands.]*

LADY MACBETH: A foolish thought to say a sorry sight.

MACBETH: There's one did laugh in's sleep, and one cried 'Murther!' […]
But they did say their prayers […]
List'ning their fear, I could not say 'Amen,'

LADY MACBETH: Consider it not so deeply.

MACBETH: But wherefore could not I pronounce 'Amen'? […]

LADY MACBETH: Why did you bring these daggers from the place?
[…] Go carry them, and smear
The sleepy grooms with blood.

MACBETH: I'll go no more:
I am afraid to think what I have done;
Look on't again I dare not.

LADY MACBETH: Infirm of purpose!
Give me the daggers.

[Act 2, scene 2, lines 9–31 and 48–53]

1 In a small group, discuss:

- What mood does Shakespeare create?
- How is the tension built up?
- What effect is achieved by having Lady Macbeth's thoughts at the beginning?

2 In groups of three, perform an extract from the script above, focusing on building the tension:

- Have one director and two actors.
- Concentrate on how the characters are feeling and the way they would deliver particular lines.
- Use silence and pauses in appropriate places to create suspense, for example 'I have done the deed *[said with relief – then pause, look around suddenly wary]* Didst thou not hear a noise?'
- Try to capture the tension between the two characters.

Review

Now, perform your extract for the class.

After watching the performances, as a class, discuss what elements make this scene effective. Why did Shakespeare write this scene instead of showing the murder itself?

Homework

Write the script for a scene involving a build-up of tension and suspense. Choose one of the following:

- One character daring another to do something dangerous or illegal.
- Four bank robbers meet after a failed bank robbery. They suspect that one of them is an undercover policeman – but which one?
  Use some of Shakespeare's techniques to help you:
- contrasting and conflicting characters
- dramatic pauses
- strong emotions (e.g. fear, guilt, etc.).

Macbeth

LADY MACBETH

Aims

- To study the character of Lady Macbeth.
- To analyse the language Lady Macbeth uses.

Starter session

In this role-play activity you will explore various methods of persuasion.

- In groups of three, take turns to play the Angel (persuading someone to do good), the Devil (persuading someone to do bad) and the person making the decision.
- Use the scenarios below:
  - Borrowing someone's homework
  - Skipping your curfew to go out with your friends
  - Deciding whether to take some money you find left unattended.

Rules

- ◆ No physical contact.
- ◆ Angels and devils only have *one minute* to persuade.
- ◆ The person being persuaded cannot speak and must listen only.
- ◆ No physical contact.
- ◆ At the end the person being persuaded must make a decision based on the most powerful persuasion.
- ◆ Swap roles after each round so everyone has a turn in one of the roles.

- In your group, make a list of all the persuasive techniques that were used giving each a rating from one to ten for how effective each technique was. Did some work better than others?
- Feed back your results to the class.

Introduction

Lady Macbeth is a powerful character who manipulates her husband. It could be argued that if it wasn't for her, Macbeth might not have killed the king.

Development

DRAMA **SPEAKING AND LISTENING   READING   WRITING**

In this extract, Macbeth has decided not to go through with the murder.

> MACBETH: We will proceed no further in this business [...]
> LADY MACBETH: Was the hope drunk,
> Wherein you dress'd yourself? Hath it slept since?
> And wakes it now to look so green and pale
> At what it did so freely? From this time
> Such I account thy love. Art thou afeard
> To be the same in thine own act and valour,
> As thou art in desire? Would'st thou [...]
> [...] live a coward in thine own esteem,
> Letting 'I dare not' wait upon 'I would'? [...]
> MACBETH: I dare do all that may become a man [...]
> LADY MACBETH: When you durst do it, then you were a man [...]
> I have given suck, and know
> How tender 'tis to love the babe that milks me:
> I would, while it was smiling in my face,
> Have pluck'd my nipple from his boneless gums,
> And dash'd the brains out, had I so sworn
> As you have done to this.
>
> *[Act 1, scene 7, lines 32–59]*

1 In a group, use the lines in coloured type to help you discuss the following:

● What feelings and emotions does Lady Macbeth play on in her husband?

● List the persuasive techniques she uses.

● What *type of sentence* does she use in her opening speech? Why?

2 You are now going to construct a 'power graph' showing the relationship between Macbeth and his wife using the quotations provided to plot the points.

For example:

Quotation 1

MACBETH: I dare do all that may become a man [...]
LADY MACBETH: When you durst do it, then you were a man.

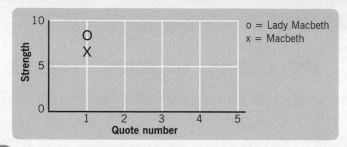

Quotation 2

MACBETH: If we should fail?
LADY MACBETH: [...] But screw your courage to the sticking-place,
And we'll not fail.

Quotation 3

MACBETH: We will proceed no further in this business [...]
LADY MACBETH: Wouldst thou [...] live a coward in thine own esteem?

Quotation 4 *After the murder*

MACBETH: This is a sorry sight [looking at his bloody hands]
LADY MACBETH: A foolish thought to say a sorry sight.

Quotation 5 *After the murder*

MACBETH: Will all great Neptune's oceans wash this blood
Clean from my hand? No [...]
LADY MACBETH: My hands are of your colour [...]
A little water clears us of this deed.

Review

Compare your results with those of the rest of the class. Who comes across as the stronger character?

Discuss what we learn about Macbeth and Lady Macbeth's relationship from the quotations. In what manner does Lady Macbeth commonly speak to her husband?

Twelfth Night

TRUE LOVE?

Aims

- To examine the theme of love in *Twelfth Night*.
- To explore how the play portrays the tradition of 'courtly love'.

Starter session

Twelfth Night opens with Duke Orsino's broken-hearted lament in which he compares love to music.

- In a small group, make a list of as many songs as you can that deal with the theme of love.
- From the list, select two or three songs that everyone in the group knows. Discuss what view of love the songs take: is love seen as painful and troublesome, or happy and fulfilling?
- Now brainstorm any typical lyrics about love from any songs that you know and write them down.
- Discuss what attitude to love these songs show: are they romantic, sentimental, realistic, overly dramatic?
- As a class, consider if today's pop songs give an accurate portrayal of love.

Introduction

In *Twelfth Night*, Shakespeare explores some of the attitudes and ideas about love that were popular in his time, such as the tradition of 'courtly love', which had existed since the twelfth century. According to this tradition, love was seen as pure and perfect, and often unattainable. In the play, Duke Orsino is 'in love' with Olivia who has sworn herself to seven years of mourning following the death of her brother and consequently rejects his declarations of love.

Development

Read the following extracts in which Duke Orsino expresses his feelings about love.

A ORSINO: If music be the food of love, play on,
Give me excess of it, that, surfeiting,
The appetite may sicken, and so die.

[Act 1, scene 1, lines 1–3]

B ORSINO: For such as I am, all true lovers are,
Unstaid and skittish in all motions else,
Save in the constant image of the creature
That is belov'd.

[Act 2, scene 4, lines 16–19]

C ORSINO: There is no woman's sides
Can bide the beating of so strong a passion
As love doth give my heart; no woman's heart
So big, to hold so much: […]
But mine is all as hungry as the sea,
And can digest as much.

[Act 2, scene 4, lines 94–102]

1 Read extracts A and B again. Pick out any words that suggest how Orsino is affected by his love for Olivia, for example 'sicken'.

- In pairs, discuss what these words reveal about Orsino's state of mind.
- Does love seem a healthy thing for Orsino?

2 With a partner, reread extract C. According to Orsino, how is a woman's love different from a man's?

- In this speech Orsino is speaking to Viola, who is disguised as a man. How do you think she might react to his views on a woman's love?

Examine how Orsino describes Olivia:

> ORSINO: O, when mine eyes did see Olivia first,
> Methought she purg'd the air of pestilence;
>
> *[Act 1, scene 1, lines 19–20]*

> ORSINO: Here comes the Countess; now heaven walks on earth.
>
> *[Act 5, scene 1, line 94]*

1 With a partner, discuss how Orsino portrays Olivia. Is it a realistic portrayal of a woman?

2 Imagine that you are Orsino. Write a short letter to the agony aunt of your favourite magazine outlining the problems you are having with love. Try to capture the flavour of Orsino's expressive and poetic style.

3 Now imagine that you are the agony aunt. Write your reply giving Orsino some sound advice. Is his attitude towards love and Olivia realistic? What should he do?

Review

Read to the class some of your advice to Orsino.

As a class, discuss whether you think Orsino had a 'mature' attitude to love. Was it realistic? What were some of the shortcomings of 'courtly love' as shown in the character of Orsino?

Homework

Orsino constantly asks for music to ease his torment. Imagine you are a musician in his court composing a love song for him:
- It may be sad, sentimental, romantic or realistic.
- It should have at least two verses and a chorus.
- Consider what images you might use to reflect the mood.
- Your opening line could be: 'I saw her light with my own eyes'.

Twelfth Night

MALVOLIO AND THE PURITANS

Aims

- To study the character of Malvolio (Olivia's steward).
- To explore the character in the historical context of the Puritans.

Starter session

Shakespeare deliberately created the name 'Malvolio' to suggest something about his character.

- With a partner, use a dictionary to look up in five minutes as many words as you can that begin with the prefix 'mal-'.
- Write down the definitions. Do not use proper nouns. Begin with these words: *malady*, *malignant*, *malevolent*.
- What does 'mal-' mean?
- From your list, discuss what meaning some of these words have in common.
- What does this indicate to an audience about Malvolio's character?

Introduction

Malvolio's character was based on a group of people from Shakespeare's time called the Puritans.

The Puritans disapproved of some aspects of the Church of England and wanted to 'purify' the Church by making services simpler and plainer. However, they were often ridiculed because of their seriousness, strictness and moralising. Puritans disapproved of simple pleasures like dancing and the theatre and showed their devotion to the Church by living simply, working hard and dressing plainly.

Development

Read the extract below:

MARIA: What a caterwauling do you keep here? [...]
SIR TOBY: [*Sings*] 'O' the twelfth day of December –' [...]
[Enter MALVOLIO]
MALVOLIO: My masters, are you mad? [...] Have you no wit, manners, nor honesty, but to gabble like tinkers at this time of night? [...] Is there no respect of place, persons, nor time in you?
SIR TOBY: We did keep time, sir, in our catches.
MALVOLIO: [...] My lady bade me tell you that, though she harbours you as her kinsman, she's nothing allied to your disorders. If you can separate yourself and your misdemeanours, you are welcome to the house; if not, [...] she is very willing to bid you farewell. [...]
SIR TOBY: [...] Dost thou think because thou art virtuous, there shall be no more cakes and ale? [...] A stoup of wine, Maria!
MALVOLIO: Mistress Mary, if you prized my lady's favour at anything more than contempt, you would not give means for this uncivil rule; she shall know of it, by this hand. *[Exit]* [...]
MARIA: The devil a Puritan that he is, or anything constantly but a time-pleaser; an affectioned ass that cons state without book and utters it by great swarths: the best persuaded of himself, so crammed (as he thinks) with excellencies, that it is his grounds of faith that all that look on him love him. [...]

[Act 2, scene 3, lines 72–149]

1 With a partner, discuss Malvolio's character.

- How does he behave and speak to the other characters?
- What do the other characters think of him?
- How would an audience react to him?

2 In groups of three, create a still life of the scene above.

- Represent the three characters: Malvolio, Sir Toby and Maria.
- Now choose some lines for each of the characters. Begin with your still life then improvise a short extract using the lines.

Maria tricks Malvolio into believing Olivia is in love with him. To woo her, Malvolio wears ludicrous yellow stockings and behaves strangely out of character. Feigning that he is mad, Sir Toby locks Malvolio away where Feste, the clown, interrogates him in the dark in disguise as the curate, Sir Topas.

At the end, Malvolio pleads with Olivia:

MALVOLIO: Madam, you have done me wrong [...]
Why have you suffer'd me to be imprison'd ,
Kept in a dark house, visited by the priest [...]
Tell me, why?

[Act 5, scene 1, lines 322–337]

1 In pairs, consider how the audience might feel differently about Malvolio now:

● How is his behaviour and manner of speaking different from the earlier scene?

● Improvise a still life with Malvolio and Olivia, highlighting these differences.

Review

As a class, discuss what characteristics Malvolio shares with the Puritans. By the end we may feel sympathy for him, but his final line is: 'I'll be reveng'd on the whole pack of you!' How is an audience meant to feel about this?

Twelfth Night

VIOLA

Aims

- To explore the character of Viola.

Starter session

Act 1, scene 2 of *Twelfth Night* begins with a shipwreck. Viola is washed up on a strange shore, believing her twin brother, Sebastian, has drowned. The Captain informs her that Orsino, 'A noble duke, in nature as in name', rules the country, Illyria. Viola decides to disguise herself as a man using the name 'Cesario' and serve Orsino as a page.

- Working with a partner, consider in what ways the position of women in Elizabethan society may have been different from society today: what roles were women expected to play; how might they have been treated differently?
- In your pairs, make a list of advantages Viola might gain by disguising herself as a man. Feed back these ideas to the class.
- Improvise two contrasting scenes showing how the role of women has changed over time. The scene should involve a husband and wife's conversation around the dinner table, first in an Elizabethan household, then in a modern home. Think about how you would highlight the differences between the two ages.

Introduction

Viola's disguise as Cesario adds to the comedy of the play. **Dramatic irony** features heavily in the scenes where she encounters Duke Orsino and the Countess Olivia, since they both assume she is a man and treat her as such.

At the end of Act 1, scene 4, we learn that Viola herself is attracted to Orsino, although she is given the task of wooing Olivia for him.

Development

DRAMA   **SPEAKING AND LISTENING**   **READING**   WRITING

Read the following extract in which Orsino debates the meaning of love with Viola.

ORSINO: Once more, Cesario,
Get thee to yond same sovereign cruelty.
Tell her my love […]
There is no woman's sides
Can bide the beating of so strong a passion
As love doth give my heart; […]
Make no compare
Between that love a woman can bear me
And that I owe Olivia.

VIOLA: Ay, but I know –

ORSINO: What dost thou know?

VIOLA: Too well what love women to men may owe:
In faith, they are as true of heart as we.
My father had a daughter lov'd a man,
As it might be perhaps, were I a woman,
I should your lordship.

ORSINO: And what's her history?

VIOLA: A blank, my lord: she never told her love […]
She pin'd in thought,
And with a green and yellow melancholy
She sat like Patience on a monument,
Smiling at grief. Was not this love indeed?

[Act 2, scene 4, lines 80–116]

Helena Bonham-Carter as Olivia, Imogen Stubbs as Cesario/Viola and Toby Stephens as Sebastian in the 1996 film of *Twelfth Night*.

1 Role-play this scene in pairs, with one person reading Orsino's lines, and the other giving Viola's secret thoughts about what he is saying at the end of each sentence.

2 In pairs, discuss Viola's last speech:

- What is the dramatic irony in this speech?
- Why doesn't she tell Orsino how she feels about him? What does this reveal to us about her character?

In this scene Viola has come to deliver Orsino's message of love to Olivia.

VIOLA: Madam, I come to whet your gentle thoughts
On his behalf. [...]

OLIVIA: I bade you never speak again of him;
But would you undertake another suit,
I had rather hear you solicit that,
Than music from the spheres.

                                               Dear lady –

VIOLA:

OLIVIA: [...] I did send, [...]
A ring in chase of you [...]
To force that on you in a shameful cunning
Which you knew none of yours. [...]
So, let me hear you speak.

VIOLA: I pity you [...]

OLIVIA: I prithee tell me what thou think'st of me.

VIOLA: That you do think you are not what you are.[...]
I have one heart, one bosom, and one truth,
And that no woman has; nor never none
Shall be mistress of it, save I alone.

[Act 3, scene 1, lines 106–161]

1 In pairs, discuss the following:

● What is the dramatic irony in this scene? What does Olivia want from Viola?

● How does Viola treat Olivia and deal with the situation?

2 Imagine you are directing this scene. Write down stage directions for the actresses playing the parts. Include:

● *how* they should speak the lines

● what actions, gestures and facial expressions they could use

● where they move on stage.

Review

As a class, recap on how Viola manages two tricky situations – one with Orsino, and the other with Olivia.

Preparing for the tests

Aims

- To look at the required skills for answering an exam question.
- To evaluate your own writing.
- To review your own reading skills and assess your strengths and weaknesses.

Starter session

The National Curriculum test question on Shakespeare requires you to write about two scenes from the Shakespeare text you have studied.

- Working in pairs, make a list of the skills that you think the question is testing.
- Compare your list with that of another pair.
- Now, as a group of four, put the things on your list into some order of priority with the most important at the top.
- As a class, discuss your findings – was there agreement about the top three things?

Introduction

In the test, for the Shakespeare question, you will be required to answer one set question on the play you have been studying.

- The question will require a detailed study of two extracts from the scenes you have studied in class.
- You will be asked to show links between these scenes and comment on how they show the ways that the characters and themes have developed.
- The question may be about the play in performance.
- The test on the Shakespeare text lasts 45 minutes.
- It is worth 25 per cent of your total grade.

The following lesson offers some tips on how to answer the Shakespeare question successfully.

Development

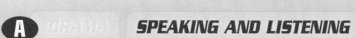

Look at the sample question below, even though you may not have been studying *Macbeth*.

In these extracts, Lady Macbeth reacts in different ways to her circumstances.

Explain how Lady Macbeth deals with the issue of killing the king in these two scenes.

Extract 1:

Macbeth has decided against killing King Duncan, but Lady Macbeth attempts to change his mind.

> MACBETH: We will proceed no further in this business: [...]
> LADY MACBETH: Art thou afeard
>   To be the same in thine own act and valour,
>   As thou art in desire?
>   [...]
>   I have given suck, and know
>   How tender 'tis to love the babe that milks me:
>   I would, while it was smiling in my face,
>   Have pluck'd my nipple from his boneless gums,
>   And dash'd the brains out, had I so sworn
>   As you have done to this.
>
> *[Act 1, scene 7, lines 31–41, 54–59]*

Extract 2:

Near the end of the play, Lady Macbeth is observed sleepwalking and talking to herself.

> LADY MACBETH: Hell is murky. Fie,
>   my lord, fie! a soldier, and afeard?
>   What need we fear who knows it when none can call
>   our power to accompt?
>   – Yet who would have thought the old man
>   to have had so much blood in him?
>
> *[Act 5, scene 1, lines 38–41]*

1 You will now practise writing about the scenes above.

- In pairs, make notes on Extract 1:
  - What aspects of character does Lady Macbeth show?
  - How is she different from her husband?
  - In what way does she speak?

- In Extract 2 she is talking as she sleepwalks. What differences do you perceive in her? How might an actress speak her lines here?

2 Use your notes to write *two paragraphs* showing how Lady Macbeth's character has developed. Here are some useful tips:

- One of the most important aspects of writing about a text is to ensure you are making points that are clearly explained and well supported with quotations. A simple way of remembering this is to use the abbreviation P.E.E.

  P – Point
  E – Explanation
  E – Evidence (a quote)

  This structure should be used for each paragraph.

- Use **connectives** that show you are aware that you should be making connections between the scenes. Here is a useful connective word-bank:

in contrast	*is different from*	*on the other hand*	*however*
whereas	*moreover*	*in addition*	*furthermore*
later on	*significantly*	*in particular*	

- Begin the first paragraph using this sentence:

  'In Act I, Scene 7 of **Macbeth**, Lady Macbeth shows what a powerful character she is ...'

- Start the second paragraph with:

  'Later in the play we see how Lady Macbeth has been affected by the killing of the king ...'

In this section you will look at how to evaluate and make critical judgements about your own work.

1 Read this attempt at the first paragraph:

'At the start, she is powerful. More than Macbeth 'cos he doesn't want to kill the King. She is stronger and makes him. She says he is a coward and would kill her own baby.'

- In pairs, consider the strengths and weaknesses of this paragraph.

2 Now read the following attempt:

'In Act 1, scene 7, Lady Macbeth shows what a powerful character she is. When faced with her husband's reluctance to kill the King she responds by ridiculing and shaming him: 'Art thou afeard?'. She is attempting to make him change his mind.

Significantly, Lady Macbeth echoes these words in Act 5, scene 1, when she is sleepwalking: 'A soldier, and afeard?'. However, this is not said with bravado and strength, but in madness. She then says, 'Yet who would have thought the old man to have had so much blood in him?'. She is haunted by the image of the dead King suggesting feelings of guilt, as opposed to her steely resolve earlier.'

- Why is this example an improvement?

3 Reread your own paragraphs. Are there any improvements to be made in style or content?

Review

Share with the class the strengths and weaknesses in your paragraphs. As a class decide on five key requirements for a successful answer to the test question.

Glossary

Word	Unit	Page	Definition
Alliteration	7–2 9–3	11 82	The repetition of the same letter or sound in a line or passage for dramatic effect. For example *the wind whistled wildly*.
Assonance	7–2	12	The use of the same vowel sound with different consonants or the same consonant with different vowels in successive words or stressed syllables. It is sometimes called 'near rhyme'. For example *bend/sell*, *mystery/mastery*, *killed/cold*.
Close-up (Film shots)	7–5	22	When the camera focuses on a particular piece of detail, usually of the character's face, to show their reactions or feelings. It could be used to emphasise anything important to the scene, for example a fuse burning, the clock ticking, etc.
Complex character	7–6 9–4	23 86	A character who is more than two-dimensional and has psychological and emotional depth that make him or her more realistic. Complex characters sometimes bring out contradictory feelings in an audience. For example Macbeth is despicable because he is a murderer, but we also pity him by the end.
Complication (Plot)	7–4	18	The part in the story where things 'go wrong'.
Connectives	8–10 9–10	70 107	A word or phrase that is used to 'connect', or link, clauses, sentences and paragraphs, and in doing so gives the ideas a logical structure and sense of direction. For example *also, besides, on the other hand, finally*, etc.
Crisis (Plot)	7–4	18	The part of the plot when things are 'at their worst', and often when tension is at its highest.
Development (Plot)	7–4	18	The part of the plot following the introduction where we learn more about the characters and the actual story begins to 'get moving'.
Dramatic irony	7–3 9–9	14 101	This occurs when an audience or reader knows more than the characters themselves. For example in *A Midsummer Night's Dream*, when Titania, queen of the fairies, falls hopelessly in love with Bottom, who has the appearance of an ass, we know that it is because of the spell that has been placed upon her.
Emotive language	7–2 9–3	12 82	Any words or phrases designed to make you feel some kind of emotion. It is used in speeches, poetry, etc.
Empathise	7–2	12	When you understand another person's feelings, thoughts and motives. When you imagine what it is like to be that person or character.

Word	Unit	Page	Definition
External status	8–4	51	The obvious status that a person or character has according to the role they 'officially' play in society. For example the king (high external status); the beggar (low external status).
Formal writing	7–9	34	A writing style that is appropriate for a formal essay, one that doesn't use slang or any colloquial language.
Genre	7–3	16	A type of play, story or film. For example romance, thriller, tragedy, etc.
High characters	8–4	52	Characters with high external status. For example the king, queen, lords, dukes, etc.
Imagery	7–2	12	Where images are used for descriptive effect to build up a mental picture in the mind of the reader or the audience. This includes the use of similes, metaphors and personification.
Improvise (Drama)	8–4	53	Where you make things up as you go along without any script or prior rehearsal.
Internal status	8–4	51	The opposite to external status. This is the inner status of the character – how the character feels about him or herself. For example are they confident, weak, shy, brave, etc. It is possible, for example, to have a character with high external status but with low internal status, such as a king who lacks confidence and courage, or vice versa.
Introduction (Plot)	7–4	18	The beginning of the story where the main characters, ideas and themes are introduced to the reader or audience.
Juxtaposing	7–7	26	Putting things close together or opposite to each other so a comparison or contrast can be made.
Long shot (Film)	7–5	22	A camera shot including objects a distance. For example focusing on a ship on the horizon.
Low characters	8–4	52	Characters with low external status. For example the weaver, tinker, carpenter, tailor, etc. in *A Midsummer Night's Dream*.
Metaphor	7–2	12	An implicit comparison, where one thing is described as if it actually is something else. For example a human pig (to describe a glutton); from *Macbeth: 'Life's but a walking shadow'*.
Panning (Film)	7–5	22	When the camera sweeps across a scene.
Personification	7–2	12	When something non-human is given human characteristics. For example *the storm bellowed with rage*.

Word	Unit	Page	Definition
Plot	7–4	18	The structure of a story; the storyline; the order in which things happen. The plot usually has the following structure: 1 Introduction 2 Development 3 Complication 4 Crisis 5 Resolution.
Resolution (Plot)	7–4	18	The end of the story where the complication has been resolved. This is not always a happy resolution.
Rhetoric/rhetorical devices	9–3	82	The art of effective or persuasive speaking or writing; artificial or extravagant language.
Satire/satirise/satirical	7–3	16	Where ridicule and irony are used to comment on an issue or genre. For example *A Midsummer Night's Dream* is a satire on romantic love because it shows what ridiculous extremes the characters go to in the name of love.
Simile	7–2	11	A figure of speech involving the comparison of one thing with another for dramatic effect. Uses 'as' or 'like'. For example *the stars shone like diamonds*; *he was as quiet as a mouse.*
Soliloquy	9–4	86	Part of a play where one of the characters speaks out loud when alone.
Status	7–5 7–10 8–2	20 38 47	The 'importance' of a character according to their social or professional position and how much they are respected (see also **internal** and **external status**).
Still life (Drama)	8–6 9–4	57 85	Where a still scene is created like a photograph; the actors are 'statues', in frozen positions, making up the scene. Also known as tableaux.
Structure (see **plot**)			
Sub-plot	7–4	18	The secondary stories that run alongside the main plot.
Symbolically	7–8	31	When something is used as a symbol to represent other commonly held beliefs and behaviours. For example the use of red as a symbol for danger, or the cross as a symbol for Christianity.
Tension	7–5	20	1. In the plot, where the suspense is built up. 2. In a scene, it could be the friction between characters.
Visualise	7–5	22	To have a picture in your mind.

Acknowledgments

The authors and publishers wish to thank the following for permission to use copyright material:

AM Heath & Co. Ltd/The Estate of George Orwell for the extract from *Animal Farm* on page 83; BFI Stills Archive for the photograph of Laurence Olivier in *Henry V* (1944) on page 73; BFI Stills Archive for the photograph of Kenneth Branagh in *Henry V* (1994) on page 74; BFI Stills Archive for the photograph of Imogen Stubbs, Toby Stephens and Helena Bonham-Carter in *Twelfth Night* (1996) on page 103; Joe Cocks Studio Collection, Shakespeare Centre Library, Stratford-upon-Avon for the photograph of Bob Peck in the 1982 RSC production of *The Tempest* on page 38; Joe Cocks Studio Collection, Shakespeare Centre Library, Stratford-upon-Avon for the photograph of Juliet Stephenson as Titania in the 1989 RSC production of *A Midsummer Night's Dream* on page 39; Joe Cocks Studio Collection, Shakespeare Centre Library, Stratford-upon-Avon for the photograph of Sue Blane's set design from the 1989 RSC production of *A Midsummer Night's Dream* on page 40; Malcolm Davies, Shakespeare Centre Library, Stratford-upon-Avon for the photograph from the 1989 RSC production of *A Midsummer Night's Dream* (1989) on page 10; Malcolm Davies, Shakespeare Centre Library, Stratford-upon-Avon for the picture of Antony Sher and Harriet Walter in the 1999 RSC production of *Macbeth* on page 89; Mary Evans Picture Library for the engraving of a map of the world on page 29; McLean Press Ltd for the engraving of Shakespeare on page 5; Popperfoto/Imperial War Museum for the photograph of World War 1 soldiers on page 79; Reg Wilson Collection, Royal Shakespeare Company for the photograph of David Troughton in the 1993 RSC production of *The Tempest* on page 38.